The Complete Book of ROCK CRAFTING

DRAKE PUBLISHERS INC.
NEW YORK · LONDON

The Complete Book of ROCK CRAFTING

by Jere Day & Linda Peavy

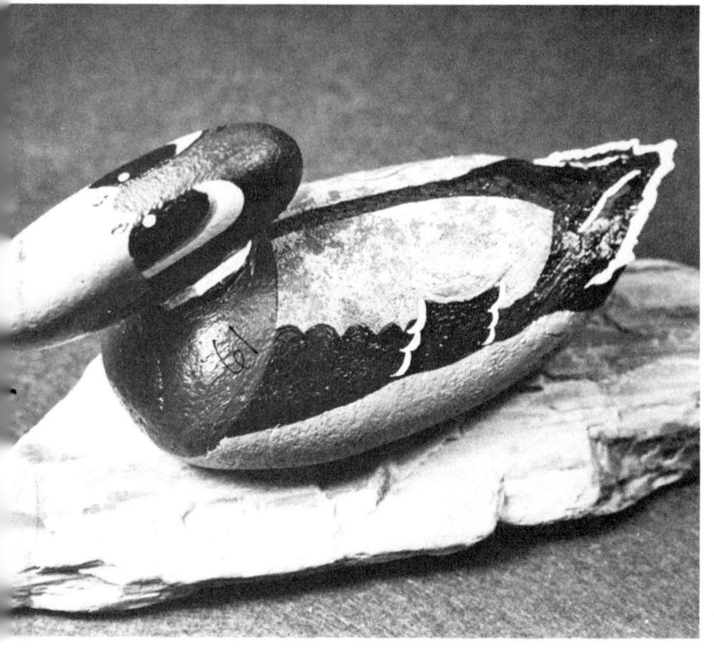

Published in 1976 by
Drake Publishers, Inc.
801 Second Avenue
New York, N.Y. 10017

Library of Congress Catalog Card Number: 75-36134

Peavy, Linda
The Complete Book of Rock Crafting.

New York Drake Publishers, Inc.

Feb. 1976 10'10'75

ISBN: 0-8473-1053-1

Book Design: Harold Franklin

Line Illustrations: Ted Enik

Printed in the United States of America

To
Gay and Claribel Sellers
and
Walter and Virginia Johnson,
the parents who taught us we could
do anything we set our minds to,
and to
Howard Peavy and Al Day,
the husbands who have always
been willing to help us try.

Contents

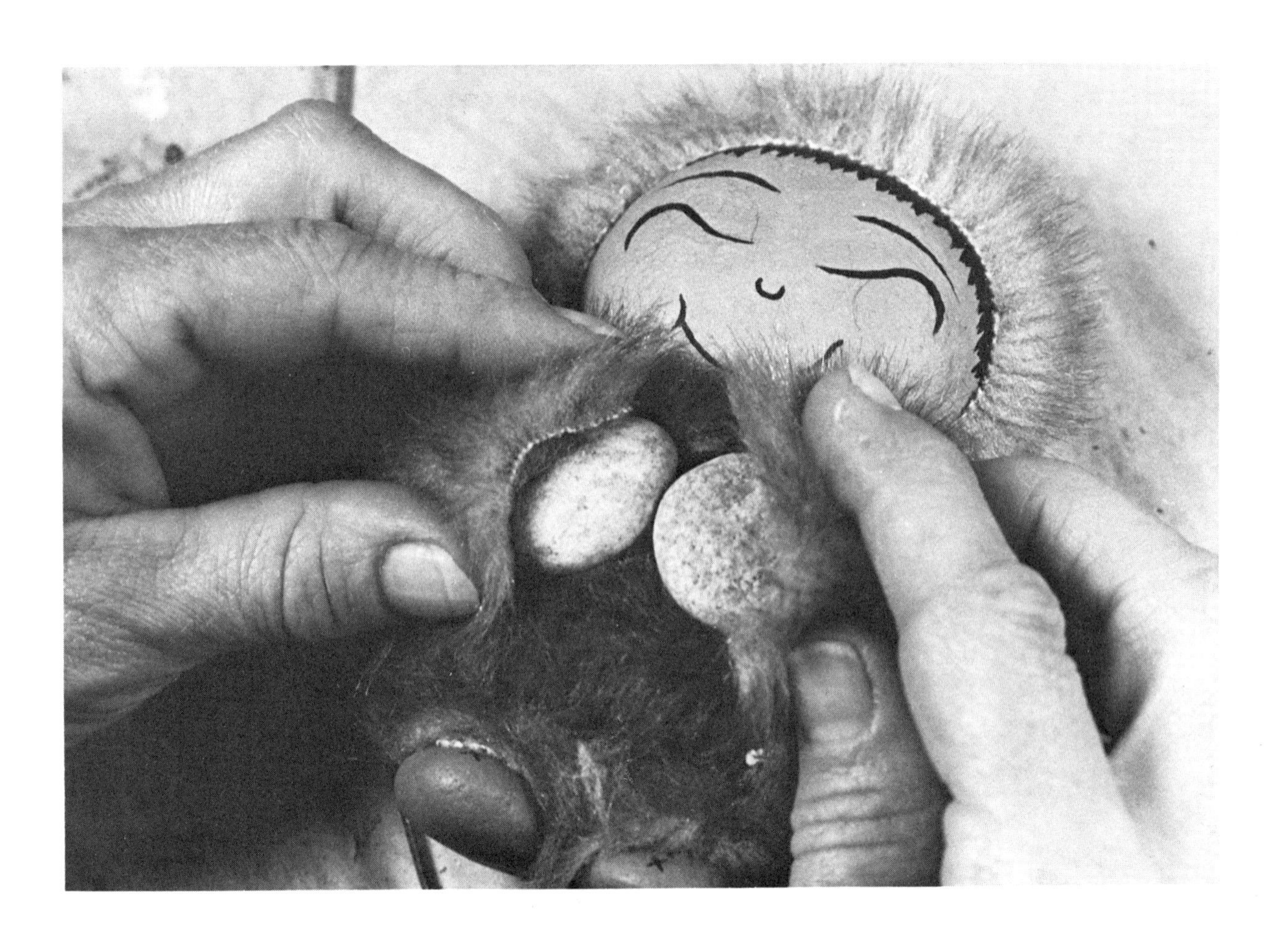

Preface

The colorful animals on the cover of this book all have one thing in common—they were once a group of rocks lying along a riverbank. A little glue, a coat of paint, and lots of creativity have turned them into lovable creatures with delightful personalities. They are products of rockcraft, one of the nation's newest and fastest-growing hobbies.

Rock animals, rock insects, rock people are appearing in gift shops across the country, and customers are eagerly buying the colorful creatures. Furthermore, they're always wanting to know more about them. Are they made from real rocks? How are they stuck together? What sort of paint has been used? How do you make this little fellow's antennae?

Designed to answer these and many other questions, *The Complete Book of Rockcrafting* has evolved from Jere Day's six years in rockcrafting. Starting in 1969 with a few small orders from local stores, Jere has built her rock art into a thriving business. She works long hours to supply her 16 outlets with the more than 2,000 rock creatures they order each year.

Producing approximately ten rocks per working day, Jere has discovered numerous time and labor-saving tricks, which the beginning rockcrafter will find invaluable. These tips, plus the illustrated, basic techniques presented in Part I, make rockcrafting the Day way an almost fail-proof endeavor for even the rank amateur. Featuring general equipment and basic steps involved in the production of a rock turtle, this section of the book introduces the beginner to the techniques of a professional.

Obviously strong on experience, Jere is also rich in creativity. Though currently limiting production to the eighteen designs she has found to be most popular with buyers, she remains constantly open to new ideas. Parts II, III, and IV provide detailed instructions on how to make some of her most popular models.

Tips on displaying rockcrafted items to greatest advantage and using rock creatures in various ways are emphasized in the book's final section, "Putting It All to Use." Photos or descriptions of rock figures used in terrariums, as wall hangings, as lawn and patio pieces, as accent figures in driftwood arrangements, and in many other ways should stir the reader's imagination in planning his or her own projects.

Whether you plan to only dabble briefly in rockcraft, to teach rockcrafting to school or church groups, or to turn rocks into gold by selling your creations, *The Complete Book of Rockcrafting* will prove an invaluable source book. After you read the book, we hope you gather your rocks and glue and paint them, use the figures yourself, give them to family and friends, or make a profit by selling them. But, above all, we hope that you enjoy making them, for that's what rockcrafting's all about.

Part I

GETTING STARTED
or
Slow But Steady Wins The Race

Part I

GETTING STARTED

or Slow But Steady Wins The Race

Basic Equipment

Neither exorbitantly expensive nor remarkably inexpensive, rockcrafting requires certain basic supplies, which, for best results, need to be of the highest quality. A realistic estimate of necessary expenses for a beginner would be ten to twelve dollars, but with this cash outlay, a rockcrafter could buy enough supplies to make a hundred or more animals. Since no beginner's kit is yet available and since most of the necessary supplies come in relatively large packages, sharing expenses with a friend seems to be an excellent way to get started with a minimum cash outlay. You may even already have on hand several of the items discussed in this section.

Rocks

A logical first on the basic equipment list, rocks are the least expensive items needed—unless you happen to live some distance from a rock source. Paradoxically, they are both the easiest and the hardest items to find. Easiest, because almost every area has its share of suitable rocks. Hardest, because finding just the right rock is sometimes a problem.

Locating the Rocks. From the rivers of Pennsylvania to the gravel pits of the deep south, from the swift-moving streams of the Rockies to those of the Appalachians, from California's rocky coastline to that of eastern Maine, there are rocks of all shapes, sizes, and colors. Many of these rocks will lend themselves to the rockcraft projects described in this book. Smooth, flat pebbles of about one-quarter inch in thickness become feet. Medium-sized oval or round rocks can be turned into heads. Larger stones become the main trunk or body of a rock critter.

Check riverbanks and dry creekbeds first, since rushing waters tend to make rocks round and smooth. If you find only relatively small rocks, try making terrarium figures. If you live in a flat area whose sluggish streams don't produce suitable rocks, ask your state's tourist bureau to help you locate rocky streambeds close to your home.

If you live in an area where no fast-moving streams are nearby, check with the local highway department to find out where they get gravel for road repairs. Chances are you can find suitable rocks at a gravel pit within reasonable driving distance of your home. If not, perhaps you could get permission to look through the highway crew's gravel stockpiles. There should be no charge for your rock-hunting there—unless you decide to take away a truckload!

Rocks brought back from family outings, weekend trips, or long vacations can be turned into items especially appropriate to the area visited. For example, rocks found in Yellowstone National Park can become brown bears, rocks from a fishing trip can be turned into rainbow trout, rocks collected at scout camp can become terrarium turtles, and rocks from grandmother's house can become colorful butterflies.

Such souvenirs are doubly treasured because they are reminders of gathering rocks at the place visited and of making the items after the trip has ended. Friends who are lucky enough to receive a souvenir you have made yourself will treasure your gift far more than the usual tourist item.

The Gathering. Whether they are found close to home or on a cross-country vacation, rocks for rockcraft items are not indiscriminately shoveled into a wheelbarrow or sack. They are carefully chosen, one by one, because their shape, smoothness, and size mean they are ideal rocks for a certain project. A rough rock of the right size may be tempting, but when you're trying to paint its pitted surface, you'll wish you'd left it on the riverbank.

At first you may not know exactly what you're looking for and may come home with quite a few rocks you can't use and lacking just the right one for the head of that dog you wanted to make. But with experience, you'll soon be choosing only the suitable ones.

In fact, as you walk along a rocky shoreline, you'll begin to see not just rocks but heads, bodies, feet, wings. Suddenly you'll spot just the rock you need for the head of that pelican Aunt Martha wanted you to make for her bird club. Or rocks that already look like rainbow trout. Or a group of rocks just the right size and shape for making caterpillars.

At this stage in your development as a rockcrafter, rock hunting takes on new excitement. Your creative spirit is at work from this, the earliest step in the crafting process. You will probably become so excited about a few of your finds that you'll carry them in your pocket rather than trusting them to one of the bags or buckets into which you've placed rocks destined for a more mundane existence.

Still, for every pelican head you'll use, you'll probably need 500 frog and turtle feet, so the bucket for feet cannot go unfilled. Having a container for rocks of various sizes makes sorting easier later and keeps you from losing some of the noses, ears, and tails you've so carefully gathered. Having to place the rocks in containers as you work also helps you avoid the urge to scoop up rocks without giving real thought to their probable use.

If your rock hunting is a family affair, even the youngest child can carry some of the smaller rocks, while larger ones can be handed to Mom and Dad. If the area is not too rough or sandy to allow wheels to roll with ease, a child's wagon or a wheelbarrow can be helpful in bringing back the really heavy finds, such as the rocks used in turtles or ducks for lawn or fireplace adornment. The wagon could also carry containers for the rocks of different shapes and sizes.

One final tip is in order. Avoid gathering rocks whose surface is coated with algae or sediment, even though this coating may seem attractive to you. Even careful washing won't remove such crusts easily, and doing a smooth paint job on a crusty rock is almost impossible. Also, while glue adheres to such a surface fairly easily, the crust of sediment or algae will usually break away from the rock, leaving you with a pile of loose or separated rocks.

Sorting The Rocks. Once the rocks are home, a more careful sorting is in order. For the really enthusiastic rockcrafter, large wooden bins may be used for large head and body rocks, while buckets will serve to hold rocks for feet, tails, eyes, and noses. If you have a smaller collection, plastic pails or dishpans will hold heads and bodies, while cut-off bleach or detergent bottles can hold feet, noses, tails, and eyes. Sorting the rocks early is vitally important if you intend to move quickly through the other steps in rockcrafting. Finding the perfect feet for a bumblebee requires some time even when you're looking through a bucket of rocks labeled "feet." The task becomes doubly frustrating if you're digging through a pile of rocks of every size, shape, and thickness.

Inevitably, you'll end up with a group you now realize should never have been brought home. Use them for a rock garden, as gravel for a hole in your driveway, or as rocks in an aquarium—but don't feel obligated to turn them into rock creatures just because you've gone to the trouble of lugging them home. In rockcrafting having the right rock is vital.

Washing The Rocks. Since a clean surface is essential for a good glue and paint job, you will need to wash your rocks. If you store your sorted rocks indoors, you might prefer to wash them before you sort them into storage bins. Whenever you wash them, just be sure you've allowed them to dry thoroughly before you start the gluing process.

Though some of your rocks may need a

good brushing with hot, soapy water, you'll find that most can be sprayed indoors with a kitchen sink spray or outdoors with the garden hose. Unless you've gathered rocks with crusts of algae, scum, or sediment, washing should be an easy job.

Towel the rocks dry, let them dry outdoors in the sun, or use very hot water for washing and let them air dry indoors.

Glue

Finding the right glue is almost as vital as finding the right rock, for all but the simplest rock figures will be made of more than one stone. Having a beautiful six-rock turtle lose three feet before the paint has dried can be a traumatic experience.

To avoid such mishaps, choose a glue that retains its flexibility, since such a glue is less likely to fail under stress than one that dries to a hard, brittle state. While a properly glued rock animal need not be a hands-off item for even a toddler, one held together with brittle glue is certain to lose a limb even with careful handling by adults only. Except in unusual conditions (such as extremes in temperature and humidity), a glue that retains its flexibility will endure the normal bumps and bangs that a young child might give to a rock item.

Rockcraft glue should be thick enough to avoid dripping and smearing. A glue about the consistency of marshmallow syrup seems to work best. Even though excess dried glue can be trimmed and is usually covered with paint, the glue should dry clear in case you want to leave parts of the rock unpainted.

There may be several glues that meet the above criteria, but the one Jere has used with greatest success is Mighty "Tacky"® (Activa Products, Inc., 582 Market Street, San Francisco, California 94104). This glue is relatively expensive, but choosing a cheap, ineffective glue represents false economy. The glue must do its job well or all other efforts and supplies will be wasted.

On other items involved in the gluing process you can economize. Applicators, while necessary, need not be expensive. Tongue depressors split in half lengthwise, popsicle sticks, or orange sticks like those found in manicure sets all make good gluing sticks.

Props on which to rest heads or other extended parts during the drying process are also needed. Use wooden or plastic, rather than cardboard, objects as props, since glue tends to stick to cardboard. While a child's wooden blocks might sometimes work, 1″ × 1″ × ¼″ wood scraps (such as pieces of lath) and plastic poker chips or dominoes seem to work best as props. By using several of these wood scraps or chips, you can achieve almost any height needed. Larger blocks will invariably prove a bit too short or too tall for the animal you're working with. Whenever possible, put a poker chip on top of a prop stack, since glue is less likely to stick to plastic chips than to other prop items.

A workboard for gluing saves messy counter tops, and the rough side of a 2′ × 2′ masonite board seems ideal. Since the glue doesn't stick well to the scored side of the masonite, you can remove your animals when dry without leaving behind a tail or foot. Also, the propped-up rocks don't slide around on the rough surface if you need to move the entire board to a better place during drying time.

A single-edged razor blade is useful for trimming away excessive glue after the rocks have dried and are ready to be painted. Careful with the razor blade, though. Even besides the safety factor, a blood-stained rock makes an unsightly figure!

A few squares of felt are useful for covering the bottoms of rock creatures whose undersides seem especially rough. All really heavy items should probably be felt-bottomed to prevent scratching table tops and floors.

Modeling Paste

Turtle tails, duck tails, bee stings, owl feathers, bear fur, and grass at the base of mushrooms all require the added touch that modeling paste can give. If you prefer to avoid buying modeling paste, however, you can make most of the other items described in this book without it.

There may be a modeling paste on the market which is of the perfect consistency for rockcrafting, but Jere has not yet found one. To obtain a product of the desired consistency, she uses a half-and-half mixture of Liquitex® (Permanent Pigments, Inc., 2700 Highland Avenue, Cincinnati, Ohio 45212) and Vanguard I® Flex-Tex (Hunt Manufacturing Co., 1405 S. Locust Street, Philadelphia, Pennsylvania 19102).

If you mix a paste, be sure to keep containers tightly covered, since the paste will harden if exposed to air for very long. Two tightly twisted plastic bags can give added protection to your paste mixture if you don't think your container is airtight.

Try mixing modeling paste with acrylic paints to produce a modeling medium as close as possible to the color that the modeling-paste portion of the figure will later be painted. Chips won't show as badly if the modeling paste is nearly the same color as the paint that covers it. Remember, all modeling paste mixtures will dry up if left in the open, so close containers tight.

Paints and Brushes

Paints that apply easily, cover well, and give a permanently bright, chip-resistant finish are needed in rockcrafting. Best suited for the job seem to be the acrylic paints available in most hobby shops.

Unlike oils, acrylics are water soluble. This means the paints can be thinned and the brushes can be cleaned with water. If water is applied immediately to furniture or clothes on which acrylic paints have been spattered, the paint usually washes out with relative ease. Once allowed to dry on rocks, clothes, or brushes, though, it's as permanent as oil paint.

Acrylics come in basic colors, and a color chart or wheel can help you to achieve desired shadings. Such charts are found in many encyclopedias, in starter sets of acrylic paints, and at many hobby or craft shops. While an artist may need many subtle variations of the shades on a color wheel or chart, a rockcrafter will usually find several color combinations which will rapidly become standbys.

Rather than mixing small dabs of these colors on a palate or card every time they are needed, try mixing larger amounts in plastic containers. If the lids fits tight, the paint will remain workable for long periods of time and that hard-to-mix shade you like for the markings on a rainbow trout or the feathers of a mallard duck will be waiting for you whenever you need it.

Even basic colors can be thinned to the desired consistency and stored in tight-lidded plastic containers, thus avoiding wasting the paint that dries on a card or palate. The paints should be checked once a week or so to be sure they have not dried out. Occasionally, you will need to add water to bring the consistency of paint in the plastic containers back to that of paint in the tubes.

Although a wide variety of brush sizes is available, a rockcrafter can do well with three sizes: a number ten, a number one, and a triple aught. The number ten (#10), a flat brush, is used for most large surface areas. The number one (#1) and triple aught (#000) are pointed brushes used for small, detailed work. A beginner might find the #000 is best for all detailed work since neatness is easier with a thinner tip. When painting skills improve and more speed is desired, try graduating to a #1 for all but the finest line work.

Red sable oil brushes wear best and produce the best work. Acrylic brushes are coarser and tend to leave a lined rather than a smooth surface.

Rocks are hard on brushes, and proper care must be taken to ensure reasonably long brush life. This care takes only a few minutes and does not really differ from the care that a painter of canvases gives to good brushes. Be sure to rinse out #1 and #000 brushes and wipe them with a paint cloth, reshaping their points as you wipe. Store them flat or on their wooden ends, for a thin brush left standing overnight in the water jar, bristles down, will form itself into a curve and tend to stay that way while you try to paint with it.

Less caution is necessary with the flat #10. Even if left bristles down in the water jar, it retains its shape. Don't leave *any* brush filled with paint—dried paint can't be easily removed without damaging the bristles, and brush life will be shortened by such careless actions.

A good working surface for the painting process is a 12″ × 18″ sheet of clear glass. A single-edged razor blade can be used to remove paint droppings and keep the surface clean so that the rock creatures can be set down to dry without picking up flecks of stray paint on their feet or backs. When an animal has dried, scrape away any paint he might have left behind him, and you're ready to paint again. Window-glass dealers and frame shops have glass that is beveled on the edges to prevent cuts. Often a window-glass shop will bevel a scrap piece for you at a very reasonable price.

Keep a container of water handy for thinning paint, and another for washing brushes. A paint cloth should be ready for wiping up spills, wiping brushes, or cleaning paint off hands.

Since some rocks are too dark to be easily covered with light shades such as yellows or pinks, a quick-drying gesso undercoating can save time and money by lessening the need for multiple coats of paint and can save nerves by providing a smoother working surface.

Spray Fixative

Rockcrafting's final step is spraying the painted item with one of the many clear plastic sprays available in hobby and paint shops. Any spray that leaves a soft satin (not glossy) finish is acceptable. This spray coating not only gives a professional finish to the item, it also protects the painted surface from scratches and protects the water-soluble glue from the effects of high humidity.

Spraying on a fixative can be dangerous if certain precautions are not taken. Read the label and follow all printed directions with care. Most fixatives are flammable and should not be used near open flames or in extremely hot, close rooms. Breathing fixatives over long periods of time can cause lung disorders and even brain damage. To avoid such problems, spray outside whenever weather permits.

If extremely cold or wet weather conditions make indoor spraying a necessity, always wear a mask and work in a well-ventilated place. Most paint stores sell such masks, and you may as well buy in bulk. It's cheaper, and you'll find the masks can be used whenever an air-filtering device is needed in household or craft projects.

Basic Techniques

Though a rock turtle serves as model in the step-by-step directions that follow, many of these same gluing and painting techniques can be used when creating any rockcraft item. Variations in design can be attempted after these basic steps have been mastered.

Choosing a Model

Models can be sketches of creatures you've dreamed up yourself, pictures from a child's book, or photographs of real animals or people. Whatever your model—animal, bird, insect, or person—your rockcrafted version of it should be a caricature rather than a realistic representation. Even an experienced artist usually has trouble creating realistic features, since the unchangeable shape of the rocks severely limits attempts at realism.

Since cartoon likenesses of your chosen model will be judged more on their originality than on their scientific and artistic exactness, even the goofs you make in creating them may contribute to their winsome personalities. Choosing to caricature rather than carbon copy nature's likenesses means freeing yourself from worries about exact coloration and correct proportion. In fact, as indicated in the section below, deliberately exaggerating certain features is the essence of caricature and can create a delightful effect.

A basic sketch of a turtle, such as the one shown here, can set your imagination to work. Look at a coloring-book turtle rather than at the live creature in your neighbor's terrarium, for the most appealing rock turtles are far from the real thing. All you really need is the basic body shape, though an especially good cartoon drawing might help you to get ideas about painting facial features.

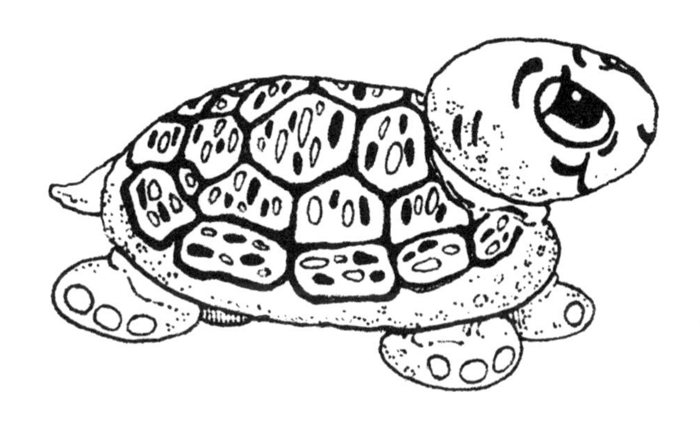

TURTLE MODEL

Choosing The Rocks

A turtle requires either six or seven rocks, depending on whether you prefer a rock tail or one made of modeling paste. Start by choosing a body, since the size of the body rock will help to determine the size of the other rocks needed.

The turtle's body should be smooth, slightly oval, and quite flat. Size and thickness will vary, depending on the ultimate use you have in mind for your turtle. A terrarium terrapin may have a body of less than an inch, while a lawn turtle's body may weigh 25 pounds or more. It's a good idea to limit yourself to this maximum, for the Day household's 100-pound lawn duck bears the name Herniatia, since she almost caused her creator a slight hernia!

The head rock, either round or oval, should have more fullness than the body rock. To achieve a caricature effect, the head should be slightly larger in proportion to the body than a real turtle's head would be. Since the painting of features requires an especially smooth working surface, avoid choosing heavily pitted head rocks.

Turtle feet can be almost any shape, but they should be relatively thin and appropriately small. Choosing feet as nearly alike as possible in both size and thickness will ensure a level, well-balanced turtle. Try positioning the body over the feet, holding it down firmly and jiggling each foot to be sure all four feet make contact with body and table surfaces. If you find one that doesn't fit well, discard that rock and look for another of the correct thickness. Sometimes you can swap feet around and find a winning combination.

The tail rock should be thin and slightly elongated, ideally coming to a point at one end. For very small turtles, making a tail of modeling paste is easier than trying to glue on a rock too tiny to work with.

While you're picking out rocks, why not prepare to glue several figures at once. Beginners might prefer to choose only turtle rocks, but more experienced rockcrafters often glue many different figures in a single session. You can prepare several now, then paint them as time permits, thus avoiding the glue-drying delay period every time you decide to work on rock creatures.

Gluing The Rocks

Once you have chosen your turtle rocks, place them on the rough side of the masonite board described in the section "Glue." Then get out glue, glue sticks, and props. Sometimes the glue is not thick enough to be easily workable when used directly from the bottle. To thicken it a bit, let about one-half cup of glue remain overnight in an open plastic container. By morning a scum will have formed on the top. Stir this scum into the remaining glue and mix until smooth.

The glue should be the consistency of marshmallow cream. Though thinner consistencies of glue will hold rocks together fairly well, most of the glue will run off so that you'll have to do more trimming, and the hold won't be as good.

First, decide on a top and bottom side for your body rock. Usually if there is a flatter side, place it down, with the more rounded side left up. If both sides are equally rounded, place the smoother side up so that painting will be less difficult.

Next, glue on the turtle's feet. Remember to try placing them beneath the body to be sure you have a good-fitting combination. Try placing the rocks at various angles until they look about right. Then, using a glue stick, apply a liberal dab of tacky to the inner top portion of each foot. Finally, place the body on top of the four feet and apply firm but gentle pressure. The weight of the body rock is sufficient to hold it in place.

Don't worry if glue oozes out onto the feet, for a single-edged razor blade can trim away dried excess. Do be sure to use enough glue to ensure a tight hold. Remember that since the glue won't stick tight to the rough working surface, your animal can be easily removed, even if some of the glue has dribbled under his feet. If the feet should stick to the board, wait until the rock creature has completely dried, then use a spatula to gently work the rocks loose from the board. Tugging upward with your hands could cause you to leave a foot behind.

Now you are ready for the head. First, be sure the props described under "Glue" are within easy reach. Then try placing the head at different angles, turning the rock this way and that until you feel you have found the best position. Try to imagine how the eyes and mouth will look from these various angles. Apply a generous blob of glue to the head rock, set it against the body rock in the chosen spot, and press it gently into place.

Since the glue should dry for at least two days, gluing more than one turtle at a time means you will have several on hand when you want to paint one for a special occasion.

If a modeling paste tail is desired, place a generous dab of paste on an applicator stick, press the stick on the end of the turtle's shell midway between the two hind legs, then pull slightly upward and away, leaving a little cone-shaped tail pointing outward.

Now you will need those props. If you didn't get them ready, you will see why we suggested that you do so. Trying to keep your rocks together while you scramble for props is a frustrating experience at best. Start with a few flat bits of wood, adding poker chips one by one until the head is held in the right position.

If time is no factor, wait a day or two until the turtle's other parts are completely dry. Then turn him over, glue the tail in place, and leave him on his back until the tail glue dries.

If you don't have the time to wait, the rock tail may be glued in place at this time by applying glue to the more rounded end of the tail and pressing that end against the *bottom* of the turtle at a point approximately midway between the two hind feet. Let it stick out to the desired length, and place the needed number of chips under it for drying support.

If you have decided to use a modeling-paste tail, now is the time to fashion that. Place a blob of the appropriate shade of paste on a popsicle stick, press the stick on the end of the turtle's shell and midway between the two hind legs, and then pull slightly upward and away, leaving a little cone-shaped tail pointing outward. If your tail doesn't look quite right, just wipe off the modeling paste immediately and try again.

Your turtle must now dry until the white glue turns almost clear—about two days. There seems to be no way to hurry this process. A batch of oven-baked elephants promptly fell apart when cooled. Apparently rapid heat-drying of this sort causes the glue to lose its elasticity. Be patient. A good glue job is an essential part of rockcrafting. Remember, if you glue several figures at once, waiting for them to dry is less of a problem.

Painting the Turtle

Now that your rocks have been glued into turtle shape, you are ready to paint a personality to match the one formed by your placement of the head, feet, and body rocks. Don't be afraid of this part of rockcrafting. Jere Day's only prior painting experience was painting walls and refinishing furniture, yet her rock creatures today show that a rockcrafter is not necessarily a trained artist. Admittedly, her first attempts were far from the professional work she does today, but practice and perseverance made up for lack of artistic training.

Trim off excess glue *before* you start to paint, but don't try to trim everything you see. Glue helps fill in the form between body and appendages. Avoid placing excessive pressure on the portion of the rock you are trimming, for too much pressure can cause the glue to give. Unless you've waited a week or more for the glue to dry, a too-heavy hand may send a foot or head snapping off and fingers may get slashed in the process. The dislodged part can be reglued, and while the glue is drying, your fingers can be healing, but try to avoid both the regluing delay and the slashed fingers: don't press so hard when trimming the glue.

Two basic turtle techniques are possible at this point, and each has variations limited only by your creativity and/or supply of paint. The dark green turtle, the more natural-looking of the two, bears various patterns on his fairly realistic shell. He is the one more likely to appear on lawns, in terrariums, or on the desks or coffee tables of people who prefer an outdoorsy rock figure. An experienced rockcrafter may prefer to paint the suggested patterns on a particularly pretty natural rock, omitting the green base coat. A beginner usually finds working on a basecoat easier, since mistakes may be easily covered over with more of the base-coat color.

The green turtle's pastel cousin, appealing to those who like the soft look in everything, can carry anything from hearts to flowers on his imaginatively painted back. Here every turtle is as different as the arrangement he carries.

Choose a dark or a pastel model at this point, and consult the step-by-step directions for the chosen turtle which follow. In either case, you will need the basic equipment previously described, and in either case you may wish to paint two or more turtles at once, since you'll have all the paint colors ready and can paint one while waiting for another to dry.

Dark Green Turtle. Since a dark acrylic usually covers rocks well, gesso undercoating is seldom necessary. The first coat of paint, in this case, is chromium oxide green, which you may eventually come to call "turtle green." Paint the bottom of the body, head, and feet first, then turn him on his back to dry for eight to ten minutes.

When the underside has dried, turn the

These seven dark turtles indicate the endless variety in shell design possible.

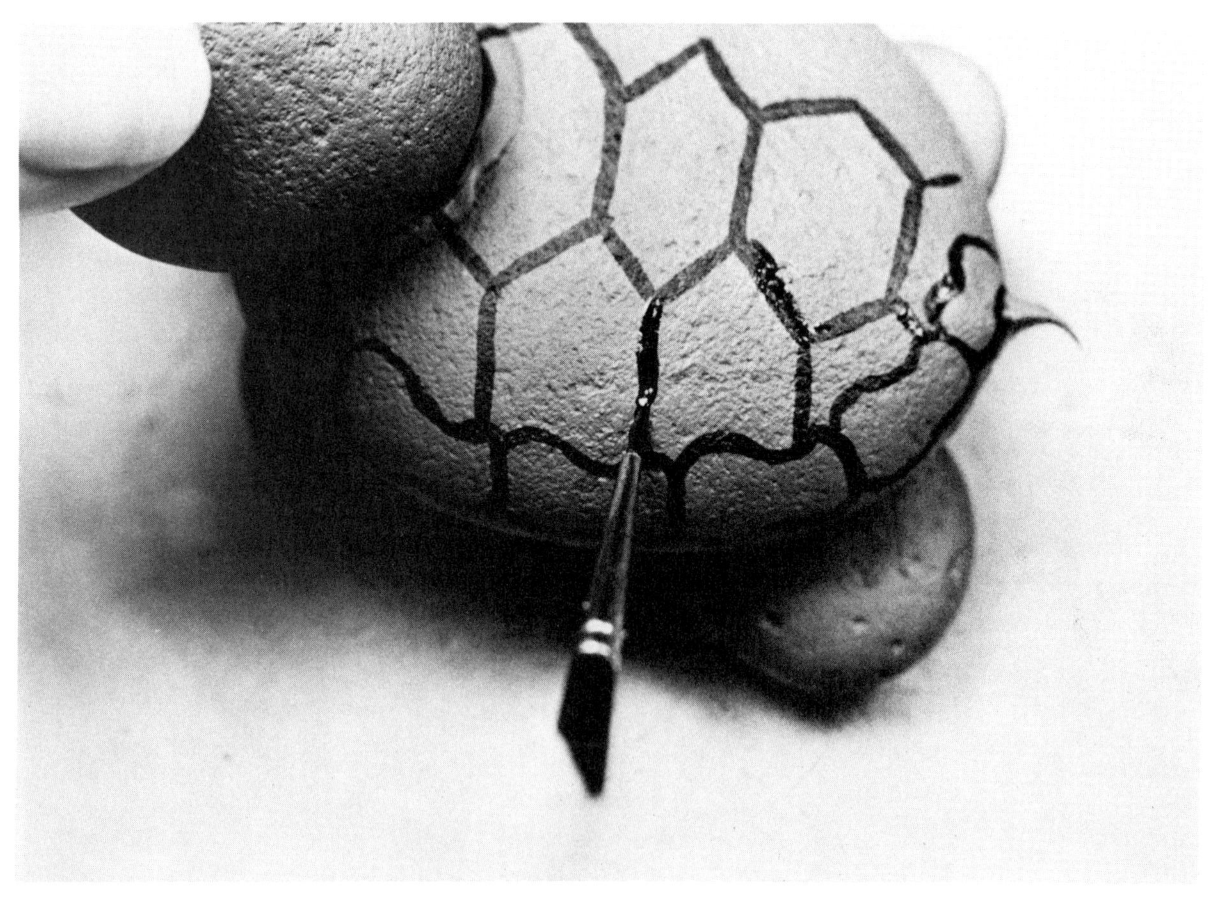

Notice how lines are drawn from the irregular rectangles of the border to meet the points of the center strip of hexagons.

This closeup shows details for a teardrop eye.

This sleepy turtle's eye is a variation of the basic "round" eye shape.

animal over and paint the top, being sure that every pitted portion, every crack or indentation is covered with a coat of green. Remember that a second coat of green can hide any mistakes you may make in the next few painting steps and can give you a fresh working surface at any time.

Using a #000 brush and thin black paint, outline the details of his back and feet. In this case, a simple hexagonal design is being created, one common to many real turtles.

First draw a thin line that curves around the base of the neck. Add other lines, as can be seen in one photo of the finished turtles, to form a slightly squashed hexagon. Join additional forms to the first one, down the center of the back toward his tail.

Next, starting at the tail, create a border of rectangles with curved top sides. Then draw lines to connect these border rectangles to the hexagons in the center of the back, thus completing the basic design outline.

While you have the #000 brush in operation, paint three small, black "V"'s on each foot. These will become toenails or claws.

Colored lines are added to the black outline next. Make sure the black outline paint is completely dry before you start to add the details. Usually the outlining on the shell is dry enough by the time you've outlined the toenails. Using the red oxide acrylic and a #000 brush, paint an orangish-red line inside the black outlines you've made. Put a "V" of red oxide inside each claw, too.

Follow these same steps with yellow oxide, being sure the red is thoroughly dry first and being careful to keep your color lines as uniform in thickness as possible. Again, don't forget the toenails.

Now a little detail work is in order. Using first red oxide and then yellow, make tiny flecks within each outlined shape. No set number or pattern of flecks per section is necessary.

Having completed the feet and back, you are ready to work on the details of the turtle's head. The eyes are the turtle's most attractive feature, and here your imagination can determine the creature's personality. Variations on the two basic eye shapes—tear drop and round are practically endless, but the open, round eye, similar to that of the terrarium turtle shown here, seems easier for beginners.

Since the eyes are a rock turtle's most prominent feature, make them somewhat larger than normal. Their position will be partly determined by the position of the head rock. If the head seems to be hanging down, for instance, place the eyes as high as possible in order to have the turtle appear to be gazing up at his human beholder. This "I'm watching you" expression is what makes these figures so irresistible to customers who see them in a shop or to friends who are lucky enough to receive one as a gift. Try placing a small dot in the place where you wish to put the center of each eye. If you use paint (*not* a felt-tip or ballpoint pen), you can easily cover this centering dot when completing the eye.

Using a #000 brush, outline the eyes in black. If you make one eye too small, just draw another line outside the first. The inside line will be covered with white and won't show. Now add eyebrows, lashes, and wrinkle lines of black.

Still using black paint and a #000 brush, add a mouth and nose. For turtles, a nose like a "U" works well. The mouth can be a simple smile line with parentheses at the ends for wrinkles. Or it can feature a U-shaped tongue placed underneath and off center, or two irregular squares, also off center, for teeth. If you prefer, make a sad turtle whose mouth turns down instead. Be sure the eyes are made sad to match by adding extra wrinkle under each eye and making the eyes look up and both to the right or left.

Wrinkles on the back of the neck are represented by simple little curves made in black with a #000 brush.

Now that most of the facial outlines have been drawn in, fill in the eyes with white. Two or more coats of white may be necessary, even if you have used a gesso undercoat.

When the white paint has thoroughly dried, superimpose the pupils on the white eyeball, using black paint and a #000 brush. Make the pupils oval or round, and be sure one side of each pupil is flush with the inside of the eyeball, giving the slightly cross-eyed look that adds personality to the figure. Again, be sure your turtle seems to be looking up at his human admirers.

When the black paint has dried, add just a dot of white to give a glint or sparkle to each pupil.

This tiny terrarium turtle's size makes him an especially appealing gift.

These pastel turtles carry a variety of floral designs on their backs.

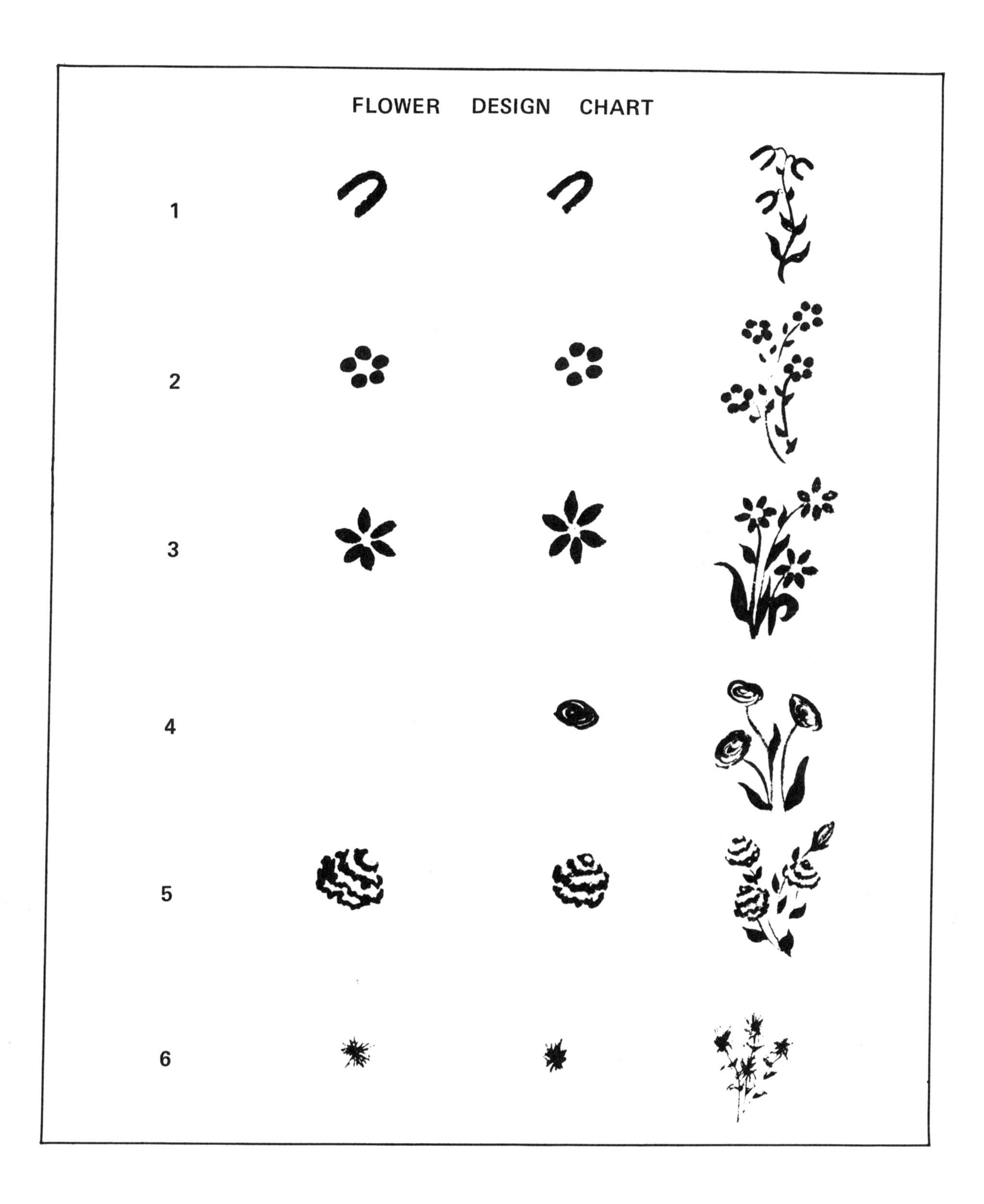
FLOWER DESIGN CHART
1
2
3
4
5
6

Can you believe it? You've transformed a handful of rocks into a lively, likable turtle—on your very first try. Or have you? Well, if you feel this first paint job is a disaster, remember that "turtle green" can cover your goofs. Hide your disaster in green, the color of new beginnings, and try again.

Once you're satisfied with the paint job, you're ready to spray your finished item. Follow the instructions given under "Spraying the Figures" at the end of this section.

Pastel Turtle. Undercoating with gesso is step one in painting a pastel turtle. If you are reluctant to invest in a container of undercoating material, you may use a base cover of white acrylic. This base coat of paint can lessen the total number of pastel coats needed, but it does not provide the smoothness obtained through use of gesso.

Begin undercoating by applying a layer of gesso to the turtle's underside. Use a #10 brush and be particularly careful to cover the glued areas between body and feet. Undercoating substances are generally very fast-drying, and you can cover the turtle's top portions almost immediately.

Next, apply a base coat of acrylic paint, a mixture of cadmium yellow light and white, for instance, thinned to the consistency of heavy cream. Be sure to let the feet dry thoroughly before starting to paint the top side. Even when gesso is used, a light shade of yellow requires two or three coats to achieve good coverage. Be patient. Each coat dries quickly, and you want to obtain a professional appearance.

Onto this basic pastel coating you can add any design, but a bouquet of flowers seems to be the most popular. Flower models are easy to find in catalogs, especially catalogs that picture crewel-work items, flowers to be painted on box purses, or flowers to be embroidered on tablecloths. Such flowers usually consist of simple, line-upon-line designs, which are easy to reproduce in miniature. The six step-by-step designs in the chart here are simple flowers for turtle painting.

As you become more skilled and more confident, you'll want to choose flowers especially suited to the person to whom you plan to give that turtle. Mums for Aunt Mary, violets for your mother-in-law,and wild daisies for a favorite niece or granddaughter.

Several different colors are required in flower painting. Pinks, yellows, violets, oranges, and greens appear in the flowers of most turtle designs. The accompanying chart dictates which colors to mix to obtain certain shades. You will need to let your own eye be the judge to how much of each color to use in any mixture.

Since pastels always require the addition of white and often call for mixtures of two or three basic colors, you will want to remember our earlier suggestion concerning storage of mixed colors in tightly-lidded containers. If you store paint in this way, you not only avoid leftover, wasted paint, but you will also be able to keep ready for use the pastels needed for flower painting.

Painting the flowers may still seem to be beyond your ability, but try these directions and see how simple flower painting can be. Always use a #000 brush, since a heavier brush cannot give the delicate effect you want to create. Thin paint to the consistency of half-and-half cream for flower painting, since thick paint will result in broken lines instead of

Napthol crimson	+ white (fairly large amount)	= light pink
Napthol crimson	+ white (fairly small amount)	= dark pink
Acra violet	+ white	= pastel violet
Cadmium red light	+ cadmium orange	= burnt orange
Cadmium orange		= orange
Chromium oxide green		= leaf green

Draw stem lines in dark green. Draw each stem in the direction each flower seems to face.

smooth, continuous ones. Keep your dampened paint cloth handy to wipe off any mistakes before the paint dries.

Starting at the center, near the top of the shell, make a small flower by drawing a series of thin lines out from a center. (See detail number 6 on the design chart.) Use a light pink here and make three or four of these flowers at various points on the shell.

When you have made several light pink flowers, use the darker shade of pink to add a center with a few strokes radiating out—the less studied and "drawn on" these strokes are, the better they will look. Stroke lightly and confidently. You'll be pleasantly surprised at the results.

Continue to build your bouquet by adding a few flowers of light orange. Make these as you did the pink ones, by drawing a series of thin lines out from a center. Then highlight these with dark orange centers and a few radiating lines.

Now add stems by drawing thin lines of chromium oxide green. Make the lines come in toward the bouquet's center.

Next, add a few green leaves like the ones on detail number 2 of the design chart. For a smaller, more delicate flower, use leaves of the smaller variety.

When your bouquet is completed, you're ready to add a border. A scalloped border can be started with the acra violet. Begin at the tail end, centering the first scallop there, then continuing around the shell's outer edge, making the scallops as uniform as possible.

You may finish the border by adding a single dot of the same color as the scallops inside each arc of the scalloping. Then add a second line of scalloping in a lighter shade of the same color between the dot and the original scalloping.

The turtle's toenails should be painted the same color as the outer scallop of the border. Use dots, rather than the "V"'s described for painting a dark turtle, since the dots give the toenail-polish effect, which such a dainty turtle should have.

Painting the pastel turtle's facial features is essentially the same process as painting features for a dark green turtle as previously described. Since the colors and design of this turtle are so soft, they suggest a feminine creature. For this reason, teardrop eyes with long lashes seem especially appropriate. Again, remember to make your rock turtle's eyes slightly crossed and be sure she's looking up at her human admirers.

When the face is finished, you have completed the painting process for the pastel turtle. If you're not satisfied with any part of your painting, cover that part with the chosen base color and start again. One turtle body can, in this way, provide the practice that makes for that professional look.

Once you are satisfied with the paint job, you are ready to spray the rock creature with a plastic fixative.

Spraying the Figures

The final step in rockcrafting is spraying your finished creation with a clear plastic, satin-sheen spray. Covering up all glued areas with the fixative is especially important, since the glues described in this book are water soluble. The fixative keeps humidity from attacking rockcraft items used indoors, and, if you've been careful to cover all glued areas with paint, the fixative can even seal out average moisture when rock figures are used outdoors.

Remember, spraying on a fixative can be dangerous if certain precautions are not taken. Read the label, follow all directions with care, use a mask when spraying indoors, and reread the section "Spray Fixatives" earlier in the book.

First, make sure there are no stray paint specks, chipped places or other blemishes in evidence. If you find an imperfection, touch it up with paint *before* spraying with fixative. Touch-up paint jobs done after an animal has been sprayed are possible, but usually far less satisfactory. Take the few minutes needed to do retouching—nothing says "amateur work" more loudly than paint specks the crafter was too careless to remove. You've done a perfect job so far. Why risk ruining it now?

Anyone who makes large numbers of rockcraft items will find that spraying them one by one is not practical. To do a fairly large group at once, work outdoors if possible. If

A dark green turtle with bright Christmas designs makes an attractive holiday candleholder.

you must spray indoors, choose a well-ventilated room (you can even use a fan) and cover the table or floor with an old sheet or tablecloth. Do *not* use newspapers, for they will leave hard-to-remove newsprint on finished objects. Place several rock items, bottoms up, on the covered surface.

Holding the can about six inches from the rocks, spray the undersides of feet, body, and head, being sure to cover glued areas especially well. Allow ten minutes' drying time before turning the figures over to be sure the feet are completely dry. Damp or tacky feet will stick to the cloth, and removing them usually strips away paint as well as fixative—right down to the rock surface. When you have placed the figures, right side up, on the cloth, spray their top sides.

Remember that fingers sticky with fixative can leave ugly prints on rockcrafted items. Clean your hands between sprayings and before handling finished items.

Stretching Your Imagination

The various pictures in this section show some of the possibilities of turtle design. The tiny terrarium turtle pictured earlier and this turtle Christmas candle should inspire you to numerous other possibilities. Try, for example, a pastel turtle with hearts instead of flowers as a valentine turtle. If you're getting new ideas already, you're well on your way to becoming a super creative rockcrafter.

If you can't possibly see how any more turtle designs could ever be thought up, don't feel inadequate—just use some of these designs until you either think of a new one you like or get so attached to one of these that you're content to paint all your turtles that way.

After The Turtle

As attractive and versatile as the turtle might be, of course, a whole world of other possible subjects for rockcrafting are just waiting to be chosen. Over the past few years, Jere Day has experimented with many rock creatures, but she has found that the figures described in the next three parts of the book plus the turtles just described are the most popular and best-selling items. Arranged in order of difficulty of assembly and painting, the models in the next sections can be made by a beginner who has mastered the basic techniques of this section on getting started.

As in the case of the turtles, all the rest of the figures are caricatures, not realistic representations. This fact greatly simplifies painting procedures, since many of the facial features are so similar from animal to animal or insect to insect that only slight variations need to be made to give a creature the distinctive characteristics that identify it as a bear, a dog, or a bee. Thus, experience gained

From caterpillar, clockwise: lazy bear, frog, pastel turtle, pink elephant, antiqued owl, fly, butterfly, bee, ladybug, gray elephant. Four in center: dark turtle, dog, ducklings, mushrooms.

in painting relatively simple features of a turtle or a ladybug can be of great help when painting the more complex elephants or ducks.

The basic equipment described earlier must, in some cases, be supplemented by such items as tweezers, narrow-gauge hobby or florist wire, or toothpicks; but many of the figures require no additional materials. Variations of a single figure are often possible, for which instructions are also given.

NOTE: We highly recommend that a beginner master the basic techniques by making at least one turtle according to the illustrated and detailed instructions in that section before attempting to make the items described in the later parts of the book.

Part II

INSECTS THAT APPEAL

Part II

INSECTS THAT APPEAL

Ladybug

Among the most popular rockcraft items, the ladybug is also one of the simplest to create. Requiring only six stones, three colors of paint, and a length of narrow-gauge wire, this delightful insect is ideal for beginners. Before trying this little creature, be sure you have read and understood the detailed instructions in Part I.

Choosing the Rocks

Six rocks are required for a ladybug. The four rocks for feet are flat and oval, very similar to those used for turtle feet. The body rock is slightly oval and thicker than the turtle body rock, and the head rock may be round or oval. This is a good place to use up head rocks too elongated for turtle heads, since placement of the ladybug's head makes elongated ovals quite acceptable.

Try several head, body, and feet combinations before settling on the most suitable one. Put the four feet in place and set the body rock on them so that the longer edges of the oval form the right and left sides of the bug. Then press down gently on the body rock and jiggle each foot rock to be sure that every foot meets both body and table surfaces. If an oval head is used, let the longer sides of the oval form the right and left sides of the head.

The Gluing

Materials. The rough working surface, glue, glue sticks, and props described in the turtle section are also used for assemblying the ladybug. In addition, you will need #30-gauge hobby or florist wire, tweezers, scissors, and two round-type toothpicks.

Procedure—Rocks. Arrange the four feet in the desired position. Place a liberal dab of glue on each foot rock, then gently press the body rock into place, remembering to let the longer sides of the oval body form the right and left sides of the ladybug.

Get props (poker chips or wood scraps) ready. Then choose the best position for the head rock, being sure the longer sides of an oval head rock form the left and right sides of the head and making sure the head angles up slightly. Note the place on the head rock where the glue should be put. Place a liberal dab of glue on that part of the head rock, gently press the head against the body rock at the desired spot, and hold the head in position until props are in place.

Procedure—Antennae. Antennae for ladybugs and other insects are formed from #30-gauge hobby or florist wire. Cut a 2½-inch length of wire and use the tweezers to twist about ¼-inch into closed loops on each end. Then grasp the middle of the wire firmly with the tweezers and bend the wire into a "V" shape. Finally, twist the two sides of the "V" to form a loop at the apex of the "V," since glue will fill this loop and help to hold the antennae in place. A final bend sets the loop at the apex of the "V" at about a 45-degree angle for convenient placement on the ladybug's head.

Antennae should be glued near the back of the ladybug's head. Break a round toothpick in two, and use the blunt end of one piece as a gluing stick to place a liberal dab of glue on the chosen spot. Some excess glue is desirable here, since it will be used to form a thatch of ladybug "hair."

To be sure the loop is filled with glue, dip the looped apex portion of the antennae into the glue container before burying it in the glob of glue on the head rock.

Using one of the pointed ends of another round toothpick, draw lines of glue out from the center blob, forming a thatch of ladybug "hair." Curls may be fashioned over the forehead, if you like.

After combing out the ladybug's hair, leave her to dry for at least two days. The white glue should be translucent or clear when the rocks are dry enough to paint.

Painting the Ladybug

Materials. A gesso undercoating agent; cadmium red, light black, and white acrylics; and #10, #1, and #000 red sable brushes are needed for the ladybug. This is in addition to the other basic equipment needed for painting rockcrafted items.

Procedure. Begin by trimming away any excess glue around head–body and body–foot joints. Work carefully, following suggestions given in the "Painting the Turtle" section.

When trimming has been completed, use a #10 brush to undercoat the head and body rocks, covering only the top edges of the feet. Cadmium red light covers best over gesso, but the black used for the feet does not require an undercoating. When the gesso has dried, use a #10 brush to apply a base coat of cadmium red light to the head and body rocks and the top edges of the feet. Allow this base coat to dry for eight to ten minutes, then apply a second coat of red.

When the red paint has dried, use a #1 brush to paint the feet black. Start where the edges of the feet meet the body and be sure the jointed areas are completely covered. If the body is very close to one or more of the feet, a #000 brush may be needed to avoid smearing black paint onto the red body. Fill in the remaining portions of the feet, including bottoms, until all feet are completely black, and allow the ladybug to dry on her back for eight to ten minutes.

When the feet have dried, place the ladybug right side up, and on the ladybug's back, use a #000 brush to outline two wings with black. A basic teardrop shape is used, with the narrow portions of the teardrop closest to the head. Try to make the wings as symmetrical as possible, remembering that you can wipe off the painted outline before it dries and try again. When the wing outlines seem the right shape, fill them in with black, using two coats if necessary.

Next, use the black paint and a #000 brush to paint the hair. Lightly brush paint outward from the center of the hair thatch, pulling thin wisps out along its edges. You may need to thin the paint in order to achieve the desired effect. Paint the Antennae wire black, too, except for the loops.

Three red spots on each wing should be added at this time. Use a #000 brush and cadmium red light to outline the dots, one in the forward portion of each wing and two in the rear portion. Fill in the outlined dots with red. Two coats may be needed to cover the black well.

Paint four dots of red on each foot to serve as toenails. Toenails for this caricatured ladybug can be painted on the outside edges of both front and hind feet.

Paint the antennae loops red; then, with the same paint, touch up any portion of the body rock's underside where you might have gotten a stray speck of black paint from the feet.

Facial features should be outlined in black, using a #000 brush. Begin by painting eyebrows and outlining the eyes. Ladybug eyes are round and have two lashes on their outer edges. The nose is an upside-down "U," and the mouth is a simple up-curve with smile lines. A tongue with two "lick lines" may be added.

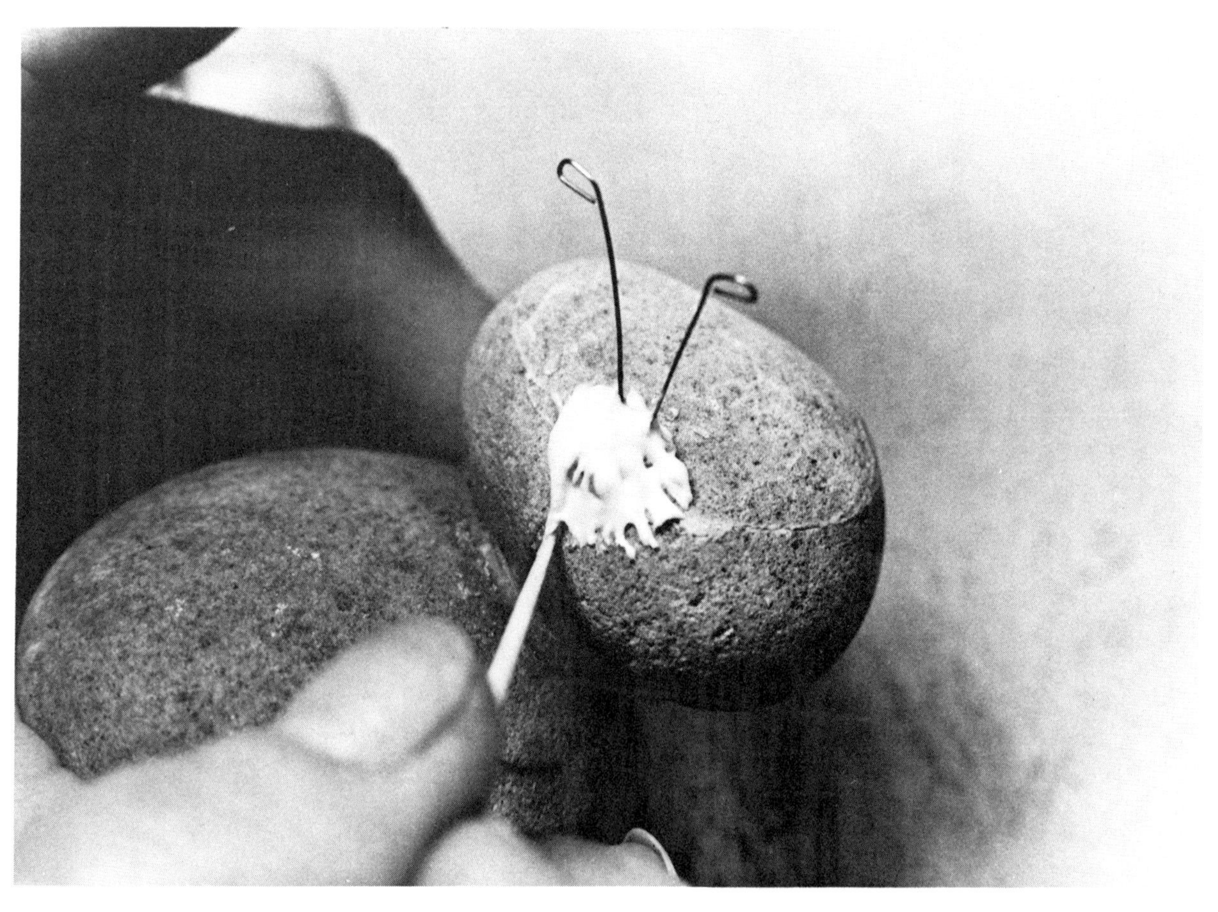

Using the sharp, pointed end of a round toothpick, draw lines of glue out from the center blob, forming a thatch of ladybug hair.

Miniature figures, like this ladybug, are favorite gifts for Mother's Day.

When these facial outlines are finished, fill in the eye outlines with white. Two coats will probably be needed. Allow ten minutes' drying time before superimposing a black pupil on the white surface of each eye. To achieve a slightly cross-eyed, looking-up effect, make sure each pupil is flush with the top or bottom, inside edge of the eye. When the black paint has dried, add a sparkle to the eyes by putting a tiny dot of white on each pupil.

Sign your name or initials to the underside, if you like. Then check the finished ladybug for scratches or stray flecks of paint. Do all retouching *before* spraying on the plastic fixative. Then, after rereading the directions given in the "Spraying the Figures" section, give the ladybug a protective coating of spray-on plastic.

Caterpillar

Caterpillars painted in "sherbet colors" of orange, lime, and lemon or in bold red and black are popular, easy-to-make gift items. Requiring seven to nine rocks, six colors, and narrow-gauge hobby or florist wire for antennae, caterpillars have simple-to-paint body designs and facial features similar to those of a ladybug.

Choosing the Rocks

Two of the seven to nine rocks needed should be chosen with special care. The head rock should be rounded in shape but relatively flat, much like a thick, round foot rock. The first body rock can be about the same size and shape as the head rock but must have a flat lower edge, since this flat edge stabilizes the entire caterpillar and prevents it fom rolling over.

The remaining body rocks should be relatively round but may be of assorted thicknesses and sizes. This is a good place to use up poor, uneven foot rocks. Choose these body rocks by arranging them in diminishing order of size, with the tail rock being the smallest.

The Gluing

Materials. The rough working surface, glue, glue sticks, and props described in the turtle section are also used for assembling the caterpillar. You will also need #30-gauge hobby wire, scissors, tweezers, and two round-type toothpicks.

In addition to the above materials, gluing a caterpillar requires construction of a simple gluing brace. Use masking tape to secure an ordinary pencil to the rough gluing surface. Then tape an object ⅜ of an inch diameter (such as a felt-tip pen) to the board about three inches in front of the pencil. These objects push up the rocks into two humps, which add to the caterpillar's appeal. Making several caterpillars at once is simplified by using two long dowels of different diameters instead of the shorter pencil and pens.

Procedure—Rocks. When you have made the single caterpillar gluing brace, try arranging the chosen body rocks to be sure they will work well. The head rock should be saved for last.

The first body rock is placed in front of the felt-tip pen with its flat edge down; the second body rock goes on top of the pen; the third body rock behind the pen, and in back of the

These finished caterpillars should be checked for stray specks of paint and retouched, if necessary, before they are sprayed with plastic fixative.

Glue the head rock gently in place and hold it there while you prop it with chips and/or wood scraps.

second body rock, and so on. When the pencil is reached, place a rock on top of it and continue to add rocks behind it until the tail rock is added. Holding the body rocks in place with one hand, try placing the head rock at an upward angle against the first body rock.

When you have decided on a satisfactory arrangement of the rocks, again set aside the head rock, for it will be glued on last. Then use the glue stick to place a liberal dab of glue near the bottom of the second body rock. Place this rock on top of the felt-tipped pen with the glue side facing the front of the caterpillar. Then place the first body rock, flat edge down, in front of the felt-tip pen and bring it up against the glued surface of the second body rock. Press the rocks gently together to be sure the glue spreads well.

Next, put a dab of glue near the *top* of the third body rock and press this rock into place behind the second body rock. Place glue in the middle of the next few rocks, treating the rock that rests on the pencil as you did the one resting on the felt-tip pen. Continue until all rocks are in place.

Now you are ready to glue on the head rock. First, get the necessary props ready. Then, remembering that the head should tilt upward slightly, try the rock in several positions, decide on the best one, and note carefully the spot where the head rock will touch the first body rock. On this connection spot of the head rock, place a liberal dab of glue.

Holding the body rocks together with one hand, place the head rock gently in place. Hold it there with one hand while you prop it with the necessary number of chips and/or wood scraps.

Procedure—Antennae. When the head rock is propped in place, fashion a wire antennae, following the directions for antennae in the ladybug section. Follow the ladybug instructions for attaching the antennae and for forming the thatch of caterpillar hair.

Before being painted, the caterpillar should dry for two or three days or until the white glue begins to turn clear.

Painting the Caterpillar

Materials. The two caterpillar body designs described in the following section can produce a wide variety of caterpillars if different color combinations are used. All suggested colors cover best if applied over gesso undercoating. The first design requires cadmium yellow medium, permanent green light, cadmium orange, white, and black acrylic paints. Design number two requires cadmium red light, black, and white acrylics. Both designs require the #10, #1, and #000 brushes plus, of course, the other basic equipment noted previously.

Procedure. Before starting to paint, trim off excess glue, using the procedure described under "Painting the Turtles." Be careful to avoid applying excessive pressure, for caterpillar sections, especially, tend to snap apart when too much force is applied.

The gesso undercoating can be applied by holding the head rock while a #10 brush is used to cover the entire body. Set the caterpillar upside down to dry, since this side of his body will touch the glass working surface in only a few spots. When the body has dried, hold the caterpillar in one hand and coat the head rock with gesso.

At this point, choose one of the designs below and follow the appropriate directions for painting the body.

Design One—Sherbet with Dots. Following the same procedure for painting and drying you used when coating with gesso (body first, then head), apply two base coats of the chosen sherbet color. The accompanying chart indicates which colors to mix to achieve each sherbet shade.

Permanent green light + cadmium yellow medium + white	= lime
Cadmium yellow medium + white	= lemon
Cadmium orange	= orange

When two coats of your chosen sherbet base coat have dried, use a #1 brush to apply scattered dots of a second color all over the body, underside included. Don't forget to dot the front of the first body rock. No set pattern is followed, but these dots should not be too close together, since more dots of another color must also be added. No dots are placed on the head.

Design Two—Red with Spots. For design number two, follow the same painting and drying technique you used when coating with gesso to apply two base coats of cadmium red light. When the second coat has dried, use the #000 brush and black paint to outline a series of circles on the caterpillar's body. Then fill in each circle with black paint.

When the black spots have thoroughly dried, lay a #000 brush of white paint gently against each black dot to make the center splotch of white.

Facial features, hair, antennae of both kinds of caterpillar are essentially the same as those of the ladybug, but the caterpillar's eyes are oval instead of round. Begin with eyebrows, then paint the outline for oval eyes, eye lashes, eye wrinkles, the upside—down "U" nose, the simple, upturned mouth with smile lines, and, if desired, a licking tongue.

When the black paint of the facial features has dried, use a #000 brush to fill in the eyes with white, using two coats if necessary. When the white paint has dried, superimpose black pupils onto the white of each eye, making sure the eyes look up at you and painting them slightly crossed, if you like.

While the pupils dry, use the base color to paint the loops of the antennae. Then add a dot of white to each pupil to give the eyes a sparkle.

Sign your caterpillar's underside, if you like, then check him for scratches or stray flecks of paint. Do all retouching before spraying on the plastic fixative. Then follow the directions and safety precautions under "Spraying the Figures" to give your caterpillar a protective satin sheen.

Flying Insects

Flies, bees, and butterflies are three variations on a single basic body shape. Requiring only six rocks, flies are the simplest of the three, while bees require the addition of flat wing rocks, and butterflies call for wings set at an angle.

The instructions for choosing rocks include special hints for all three variations as well as notes for the basic body shape. Follow the directions below to make the flying-insect body, then go on with the steps prescribed for your chosen variation on this basic insect body.

The fly, bee, and butterfly are three variations on a single basic shape.

Choosing the Rocks

Six rocks are needed for a flying insect. The four rocks for feet are flat and oval, similar to those for ladybug and turtle feet. The head rock can be round or oval, and the body rock should definitely be oval—as nearly egg-shaped as possible.

Test your chosen body and foot rocks by putting the four feet into place, setting the body rock on them so that the longer sides of the oval form the head and tail of the insect, pressing down gently on the body rock and jiggling each foot to be sure that every foot rock meets both body and table surfaces. If an oval head rock is used, let the long ends of the oval form the lower front and upper rear sides of the insect's head.

Since no gesso or acrylic will be used to cover the body and head rocks of the fly, these two rocks should be closely matched in color and texture. It is not difficult to find matching rocks in a single locality. Choose rocks of a light shade of gray for a fly, since the plastic spray finish will turn unpainted dark rocks almost black, thus obliterating facial features and wing outlines.

The bee calls for two closely matched wings of the size and shape of foot rocks. Since these will be painted black, they need not be alike in color.

Butterfly wings are thin, flat, and almost triangular in shape, though the three angles are rounded, not distinct. A flat edge is desirable along one edge, since this side of each triangle will be glued to the butterfly's body rock.

The Gluing

Materials. The rough working surface, glue, glue sticks, props, #30-gauge hobby wire, tweezers, scissors, and two round toothpicks are needed when gluing these three flying insects.

Procedure—Rocks. Arrange the four feet in the desired position. Place a liberal dab of glue on each foot rock, then gently press the body rock into place, remembering to let the longer sides of the oval body rock form the left and right sides of the insect.

Get props (chips or wood scraps) ready. Then choose the best position for the head rock, making the longer sides of the oval head rock the lower front and the upper rear of the head so that the head angles up slightly. Note the place on the head where the glue should be put.

Place a liberal dab of glue on that part of the head rock, gently press the head against the body rock at the desired spot, and hold the head in position until props are in place.

Procedure—Antennae. When the head rock is propped in place, fashion wire antennae, following the directions for the ladybug antennae. Also follow the ladybug instructions for attaching the antennae and for forming the thatch of hair.

Since you may wish to try all three flying insect variations, why not glue several figures at once. Remember to let them dry for at least two days or until the white glue is nearly translucent before painting them.

Procedure—Wings. Bee wings are added after the bee is painted, but butterfly wings should be added after the body glue has dried but before the body is painted.

Get props ready. Apply *very* thick glue to the flat edge of the wing. Then gently press the wing against the middle of one side of the body at about a 45-degree angle. Prop this wing in place and glue on the other one in the same manner.

Then, using a toothpick, spread the excess glue along the body and along the top and bottom sides of the wing. This should ensure an adequate securing of the body–wing joint and should prevent the formation of unsightly lumps of glue on body or wing.

Be sure to allow the glue on the wings to dry *thoroughly* so they will not droop when the props are removed.

Procedure—Stingers. Stingers of modeling paste are needed for flies and bees and should be added after the body, head, and foot rocks are in place. Add black acrylic paint to the modeling paste mixture, since stingers of flies and bees will later be painted black. For aid in choosing necessary materials, see the suggestions under "Modeling Paste" in Part I.

The procedure for fashioning modeling-paste stingers is essentially that for fashioning modeling-paste turtle tails. Place a blob of the black paste on a popsicle stick, press the stick on the end of the insect's body rock midway between the two hind legs, then pull slightly up and away, leaving a little cone-shaped stinger pointing outward. If the stinger doesn't look quite right the first time, repeat, taking care not to smear any paste on the body rock. Be especially careful to avoid getting excess paste on the unpainted surface of the fly's body.

Painting The Bugs

Painting materials and procedures for flies, bees, and butterflies are given in the three sections below. When the insects are ready to spray with plastic fixative, refer to the instructions under "Spraying The Figures" in Part I.

The Fly. The fly's unpainted body and head allow you to display particularly attractive rocks in their natural state, but great care must be taken when painting facial features, wings, and feet, since you cannot paint over a mistake with base-coat color. If you should make a really serious goof, you can apply several coats of yellow and move on to the instructions for a bee!

Since no base coat is used, only black and white acrylics, #000 and #1 brushes, and the general painting accessories described under "Paints and Brushes" are needed for a fly.

Before starting to paint, trim off excess glue. Be especially careful to remove unsightly blobs on the fly, since no base coat will hide its jointed areas.

Using a #1 brush and black paint, cover the feet. Start where the edges of the feet meet the fly's body and be sure the jointed areas are completely covered. If the body rock is very close to one or more of the feet, a #000 brush may be needed to avoid smearing black paint onto the body rock. Fill in the remaining portions of the feet (including bottoms) and allow the fly to dry on his back for eight to ten minutes.

When the feet have dried, use a #000 brush and black acrylic to outline the wings. Notice in the photo of the three flying insects the unusual shape of the wings. If a mistake is made in wing shape, you may be able to enlarge the outline slightly so that the error will be on the inside of the wing, the portion that will be covered with white paint.

When the outlines have dried, fill in the wings with white and add second coat when the first has dried. Additional coats may be needed, especially if you are covering mistakes made in the outline.

Using a #000 brush and black paint, draw in the four wing segments. As the picture shows, there should be three segments on the forward half and one on the rear. While you have the black paint in use, paint the modeling paste "stinger," the thatch of hair, and the antennae, but do not fill in the antenna loops.

Black dots can now be placed on the unpainted portions of the fly's body, and white dots can be added when these have dried. Using the #000 brush, outline facial features in black, following the instructions for ladybug features given toward the end of the ladybug section.

When you add the final dot of white to the fly's eye, add four white toenail dots to each foot and fill in the antenna loops with white. Then check carefully to see whether the wings need white paint touch-ups or whether the feet need to be retouched with black.

Sign your name or initials, and you're ready to finish your fly with plastic spracy fixative, being careful to observe all safety precautions.

The Bee. The bee's body structure is basically that of the fly, but he has rock wings, which are added after the rest of the bee is completely painted.

In addition to black and white acrylic paints, the bee requires an undercoating of gesso and a base coat which is a mixture of cadmium yellow medium and yellow oxide. Use #10, #1, and #000 brushes and the basic painting materials described under "Paints and Brushes" in Part I.

Using a #10 brush, apply a gesso undercoat to body and head rocks. Since no gesso is needed for the feet, you may allow the bee to dry on its feet. Then use a #10 brush to apply the bright yellow base coat to body and head rocks, using two coats if necessary.

Next, paint the feet black, using a #1 brush, starting at the edge of the feet where they meet the body rock and making sure the jointed areas are completely covered. If the body rock is very close to one or more of the feet, a #000 brush may be needed to avoid smearing black paint onto the body's yellow base coat. The yellow may be retouched later if smearing does occur.

The stinger and rings should be painted next. Using a #000 brush, paint the modeling-paste stinger, being sure the base of the stinger forms a neat circle of black. Using this circle as your guide, start a line at the top of the bee's rear end about ¼ inch from the circle at the stinger's base, depending on the size of the bee. Bring the line around to the left, taking care to keep it as nearly the same distance from the stinger's base as possible and stopping just below the stinger.

Then, redip your brush in black paint and start at the top again, this time bringing the line around to the right until it meets the first half at a point just below the stinger. Repeat this procedure with two additional lines, remembering that a coat or two of yellow base color can hide your mistakes if you have trouble keeping the lines even.

Next, the antennae, hair, and facial features should be painted, following the instructions for the ladybug face, but using oval eyes instead of round ones.

Four dots of yellow form the toenails on each foot, and yellow should be used to fill in the antennae loops.

Wings, made of two foot rocks of approximately the same size, should be stuck on a strip of masking tape, then painted black. Be sure to paint the edges as well as the tops, bending the tape away from the wings in order to get as far under each wing as possible. If you are making several bees, paint several pairs of wings at once.

When the wings are thoroughly dry, place a liberal dab of glue on each one, then gently press each wing into place. If necessary, use a #000 brush to retouch tops and edges of the wings with black, being careful not to get black paint on the yellow body.

Allow the wings to dry for at least a day, then check the bee all over for chips, stray specks of paint, or other imperfections. Touch these up and sign your name or initials on the bee's underside before applying the plastic spray finish. Remember to take necessary safety precautions when you do the spraying.

The Butterfly. The butterfly's colorful wings set it apart from all other flying insects described in this book. Glue on the wings according to the instructions under "Procedures—Wings" in this section. Allow adequate time for the glue to dry, then paint the butterfly by following the instructions below or creating your own wing design.

The materials you will need are gesso undercoating, black and white acrylics, #10, #1, and #000 brushes, plus the other basic painting accessories described under "Paints and Brushes." In addition, consult the accompanying color chart for the acrylic paint mixtures needed if you carry out this particular butterfly design.

Cadmium light yellow + white	= light yellow
Cadmium orange + cadmium red light	= burnt orange
Phthalocyanine green + white	= turquoise
Napthol ITR crimson + white	= hot pink

Begin by using a #10 brush to cover the entire butterfly with gesso. Start with the feet and undersides of the body and head. Allow the butterfly to dry on its back for eight to ten minutes, then gesso all upper surfaces. Do not gesso antenna wire, since gesso makes the wire appear too thick for antennae. When the gesso has dried, use the #10 brush to apply two coats of light yellow acrylic base color to the entire insect.

When the base coat has dried, use a #000 brush to *outline* each wing in black. Refer to the photo of the three flying insects at the beginning of this section. Don't paint in any of the interior wing design yet. Make the outer line especially thin, coming as close to the edge of the rock as possible to leave ample room for the wing design. Notice that the section nearer the head is the larger one. If you make an error in drawing this outline, you can hide the error line with burnt orange or light yellow, but several coats will be needed to cover such a line.

While the black wing outlines are drying, use the #000 brush and black paint to do the butterfly's hair and antennae except for the loops.

Using a #1 brush and burnt orange, fill in the two segments of each wing, using as many coats as necessary. Then use a #000 brush and black paint to outline three petal-shaped sections in the larger segment and two petal-shaped sections in the smaller segment of each wing.

Fill in these petals with turquoise, using at least two coats. Next, place a round spot of turquoise in the burnt orange outer portion of each wing, positioning the spots as shown in the drawing. Use the #000 brush to add a random sprinkling of smaller black dots to the burnt orange outer segments and to add three

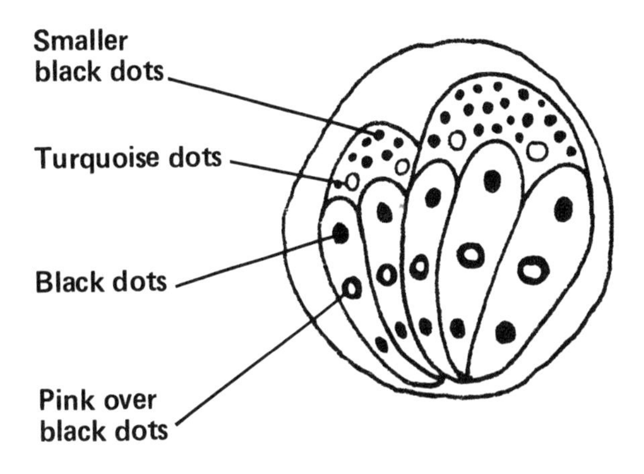

black spots to each turquoise petal. Finally, use the #000 brush to superimpose a hot pink dot on the middle black spot in each petal.

The antennae loops should be filled in with this same hot pink color, and four pink toenail dots added to each foot.

Since the butterfly's facial features are essentially those of the ladybug, the instructions in the ladybug section should be used when painting the face.

Use the #000 brush and black paint to add the tail, a simple inverted "V" with slightly curved sides. Sign your name or initials in black to the butterfly's underside.

Check the entire butterfly for chips, stray flecks of paint, and other blemishes and retouch wherever necessary before applying the plastic spray finish. Observe all safety precautions when doing the spraying.

Part III

FRIENDS

—FURRED, FEATHERED, AND FUNGUS

Part III

FRIENDS—FURRED, FEATHERED, AND FUNGUS

Dog

A rock dog can be long and lanky or short and stubby. He can have colors and patterns that approximate those of a favorite pet or he can be made of unpainted rocks. His tail can point upward in a wagging position or droop between his hind legs. From the "Heinz 57" rock pooch to the pedigree facsimile, rock dogs are easy-to-make items with great appeal.

These dogs have matching ears and feet whose colors complement the shades found in their natural body and head rocks.

Choosing the Rocks

Ten rocks are needed for a dog. Choose the body rock first and pick the others to fit its size, shape, and, if you're going to leave the main parts unpainted, color. When matching colors, remember that spray fixative tends to darken rocks and bring out their grain. Since wetting the rocks with water or licking them seems to have a similar, through temporary, effect, the easiest way to be sure head and body rocks match is to compare them when they are wet.

Almost any shape will serve for a dog's body rock, though a completely round rock would make a rather bloated canine! A relatively thick, oval rock with a flat underside works especially well.

The head rock should be slightly oval, with the longer sides of the rock becoming the muzzle and top of the dog's head. Try out several head rocks, remembering that the longer sides of the body rock will become the left and right sides of the dog. When experimenting with possible head rocks, keep in mind that dogs' heads usually look best when tilted upward.

Rocks for the hind paws are a bit longer than those for the front paws. Foot rocks can be painted in a color that complements the natural shades of head and body rocks and so need not be matched in color, even if you intend to create a natural-finish dog.

Two ear rocks are needed, and, aside from being relatively thin, these may be almost any size and shape—provided they form a matching pair. The pair you find may even suggest the kind of personality or pedigree of the pooch you'd like to build. For a natural-finish dog, if you can't find ear rocks that match each other and go well with the colors of body and head rocks, you can paint the ears to match the feet.

The round button-nose rock will be painted black, unless you prefer to paint a pinkish-brown nose for a light or blond dog. The elongated tail rock may be either painted to match the foot rocks or left natural.

The Gluing

Materials. The rough working surface, glue, glue sticks, and props described in the turtle section are also used for assembling the dog.

Procedure. Place the four foot rocks so that the longer pair forms the rear paws. Angle all four rocks outward slightly, as shown in the photographs. Let utility, not esthetics, be your guide, since achieving a good base on which the body rock will rest is more important than having the paws form a precise pattern.

Try placing the body rock on the paws, remembering to let the elongated ends form front and back of the dog. Since the head of the dog will project forward, the dog will tend to tip on his nose unless the front feet are placed near the front edge of the body rock. Press down gently on the body rock and jiggle each foot rock to be sure that each foot meets both body and table surfaces. Rearrange the foot rocks to achieve the best combination. When satisfied with the fit, place a generous blob of glue on each foot rock and press the body rock carefully and firmly into place.

Get wood scraps and chips ready for propping. Then decide on the best position for the head rock, remembering that the ends of the oval should become the dog's muzzle and crown and that the head should be tilted upward slightly. Apply a generous blob of glue to the head rock and press it gently into place, adding chips until the desired tilt is achieved.

If you are gluing many dogs at once and are not anxious to paint them right away, allow overnight drying before adding ears, nose, and tail. If you work carefully, however, you can complete all gluing in a single session.

The narrowest portion of the ear rocks should be placed at the top, with the wider part down. Try placing the ears toward the back of the head, leaving enough space between them for the eyebrows. They may be tilted outward and slightly backward, as they would tend to hang if the dog were looking up. Apply a dab of glue to one ear, press it firmly into place, and secure it with props. Repeat for the second ear, making sure the tops of the two ears are at approximately the same height. Use a finger to wipe excess glue from the tops of the ears, especially if the head rock will be left unpainted.

The button nose is now placed near the tip of the head rock. Be sure the nose is on top

Note how the sad eyes of this hound seem to gaze up at you.

This bassett hound, Brittany spaniel, and dachshund were all modeled after pets.

of the muzzle, not at its outer edge. A generous dab of thick glue should serve to hold the nose in place without propping.

The tail may be glued straight up, up and wagging to one side, straight down, or down and wagging to one side. Use a dab of thick glue to secure the tail in the desired position, then prop it to prevent its sliding out of place.

Allow the dog to dry for several days or until the glue turns clear before trimming or painting him.

Pooch Painting

Begin by trimming any excess glue around ears, nose, tail, and feet. Then choose either the natural dog or a fully painted one and follow the appropriate directions, which follow.

Materials. Consult the "Paints and Brushes" section for the basic equipment needed for painting all rockcrafted animals. Though a #10 red sable brush will be needed if you're painting a very large dog, #1 and #000 brushes are adequate for small dogs. In addition to the black and white acrylic needed for all dogs, red oxide, raw sienna, burnt sienna, and yellow oxide may be used to achieve the desired color pattern for a rockcrafted dog.

The Natural Dog. Unless you've been fortunate enough to find matching foot rocks, begin by choosing a foot color that picks up one of the predominate colors in the body or head rock. Usually black goes well with any rock, but bronze or reddish shades may be more appropriate for some dogs.

Working carefully to avoid getting paint on the underside of the body rock, use a #1 or a #000 brush to paint the tops of the feet, then the sides and bottoms. Allow the dog to dry on his back and apply a second coat if necessary.

Paint the tail and ears to match the feet, unless you prefer to leave them unpainted. When painting the ears, start at the top, move to the underside, then to the edges, and finally to the outside part of the ears.

The dog's facial features are now painted, starting with eyebrows placed in the space between the ears. Use a #000 brush and black paint to draw these brows and to outline a pair of long, oval eyes beneath them. Two eye wrinkles give the dog the "hound" touch. If you're making a black nose, paint it at this time, being careful to avoid getting black paint on the natural rock surface. A pink nose can be painted when you mix pink paints for the paw pads.

Five whisker dots are placed on each side of the nose, and a mouth line is drawn on. If the rock has a natural edge on which the mouth can run, follow that edge, making a dip in the middle of the mouth line, then curving the ends slightly downward, since hounds aren't usually happy-looking. Two wrinkle lines (like parentheses pointing out) should be placed at each end of the mouth line.

Next, fill in the eyes with white. Since no base coat has been used, you may need four or five coats. Between coats, work on the claws. Four white claws should adorn each foot, and since placement of these claws will indicate the direction in which each foot turns, try for interesting and/or realistic placement. Each claw is a single line, wider at the top than bottom. To achieve this effect, apply pressure to the brush at the top of each line, releasing that pressure as you move downward.

Black pupils, slightly crossed and looking upward, are next drawn. Remember if your dog's head tilts upward, the pupils will rest near the bottom of each eye. If you want to cross the eyes, allow the inner edges of each pupil to touch the inner edge of the eye outline. When pupils have dried, superimpose a dot of white to add a sparkle to each eye.

The pads of the feet are added last, since the pink pads tend to pick up dark paint and scratches if done earlier. Using "paw-pad pink" (crimson red mixed with a little white), outline the large rear pad, making its shape similar to that of the foot rock on which you're currently painting. Then outline four smaller circular pads out from the first, as shown in the photograph. The four dots of each pad should be in approximately the same position as the four claws on the top of the paw. Fill in the outlines in pink.

If you're painting a pink nose, place a dab of paw-pad pink on a paper plate and add small amounts of burnt umber and white until you achieve the desired flesh color. Apply this to the nose with a #000 brush or a #1 brush, being careful to avoid smearing pink onto the natural head rock.

Check for blemishes and/or stray specks

Paw-pad pink (crimson red + white) is used to outline and paint four pads. Add your name to one, if you like.

of paint, retouch, and then spray on a plastic fixative, following the directions and safety precautions given under "Spraying the Figures." One coat of fixative, applied smoothly and evenly, is usually enough to protect the dog without giving him a plastic appearance and destroying the natural effect of the unpainted rocks. Apply a second coat if necessary, but not a third. Since crimson red, even in a mixture, runs if sprayed heavily, be especially cautious when spraying the bottoms of the dog's feet.

The Fully Painted Dog. The basset hound, Brittany spaniel, and dachshund in the photos suggest the almost endless possibilites to be explored in painting dogs. You may choose to approximate the color and markings of a favorite pet, create a pedigree pooch, or just make a friendly stray. Therefore, after a few remarks about painting the base coat, we'll refer you back to the section on the natural dog for completing the kind you choose. While many dogs may be created with rocks alone, poodles, Afghan hounds, and other long-hairs require the use of modeling paste.

If you're painting a light-colored dog, begin by applying a coat of gesso. For most dogs, you should apply the primary color to body and head rocks, adding spots and splotches of a secondary color to either or both after the base coat has dried. Ears, tail, and feet may match body and head, may be painted in the second color, or may be painted black. Refer to the section on the natural dog for tips in painting these areas. The nose and other facial features are basically the same as those described above for the natural dog, as are the paw pads.

Whether you've chosen to display the natural color and texture of particularly beautiful rocks or to duplicate the color and markings of a favorite pet, your rockcrafted dog should be a delightful addition to your home or that of a friend or customer.

Frog

Rockcrafted frogs of many different sizes all have the same basic design. Make a 20-or-30 pound frog to perch on the edge of a goldfish pond, try a smaller one for indoors, or a miniature to use as a terrarium figure or as an accent piece in a mushroom grouping. Choose rocks of the appropriate size for your particular project, and follow the instructions given below.

Choosing the Rocks

Eight rocks are needed for a frog, plus one small oval rock for the ladybug perched on its nose. The body rock, basically round, should be tapered so that the front end is thicker than the rear. This gives the sitting frog his characteristic, sloping appearance. The head rock should be oval, with the shorter sides of the oval forming the left and right sides of the head.

The four feet should be somewhat triangular in shape. They may be either thick or thin but should all be of approximately the same thickness. The two eye rocks should be round, but a single flattened edge where eye meets head rock makes gluing easier. The frog is cuter when pop-eyed, so the eye rocks should be larger than normal in proportion to the head.

The Gluing

Materials. The rough working surface, glue, glue sticks, and props described in the turtle section are also used for assembling the frog.

Procedure. Place the foot rocks together so that the four points of the triangles almost touch. Place the body rock on the foot rocks, being sure the thicker section of the rock forms the front of the frog's body. Since the head of the frog will project forward slightly, the frog will tend to tip forward unless the front feet are placed near the front edge of the body rock. Press down gently on the body rock and table surfaces. Rearrange the foot rocks to achieve the best combination. When satisfied with the fit, place a generous blob of glue on each foot rock and press the body rock carefully and firmly into place.

Get chips and wood scraps ready for propping. Then try positioning the head rock so that its elongated ends form the front and back of the head. Apply a blob of glue to the head rock and press it into place.

This finished frog is ready to be checked for stray specks of paint or other blemishes, retouched, and given his protective satin-sheen finish.

The frog's eyes are glued on the highest part of its head. They should nearly touch each other, and they may actually touch if the head rock is too small to allow for space between them. Place a generous blob of thick glue on each eye rock and press the rocks into place. Since no props will be used, be sure your glue is thick enough to ensure a firm hold. If your glue is a bit thin, hold the eye rocks in place a few minutes until the glue sets well enough to hold the eyes without slipping. Wiping away excess glue around the eyes with your index finger now is easier than trying to trim dried glue with a razor blade.

The ladybug will be glued on after the frog has been painted. Allow the frog to dry for several days, or until the glue turns clear, before starting the painting.

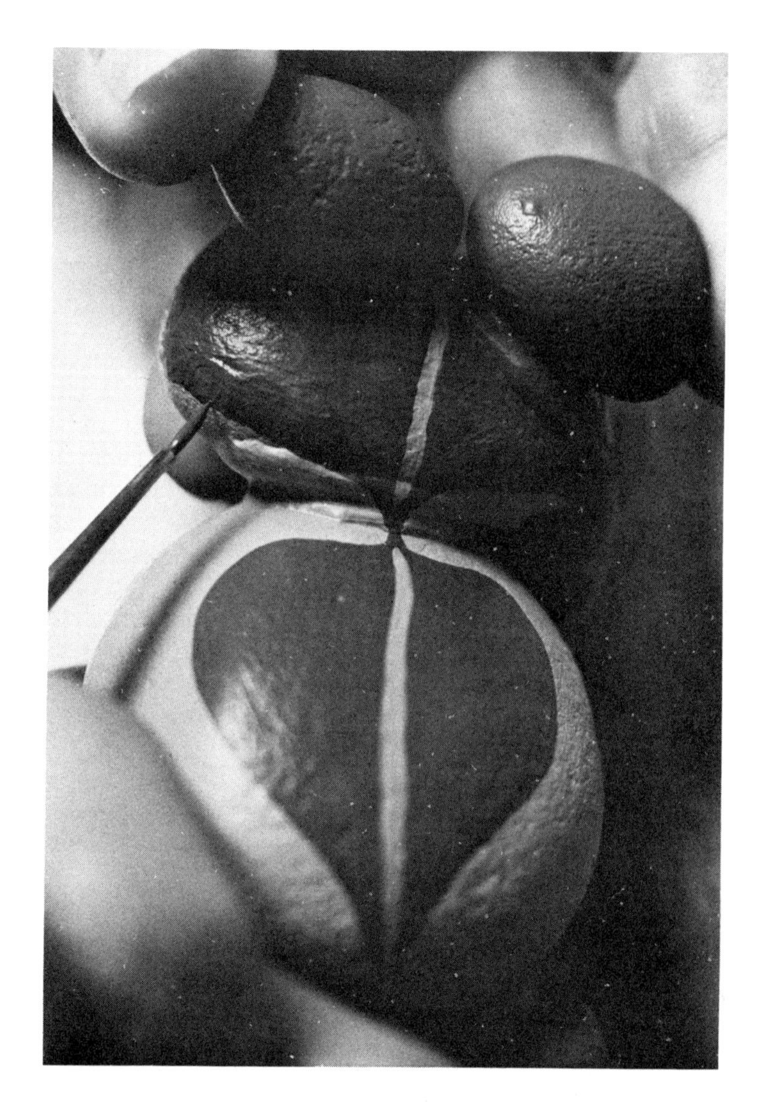

Half ovals of chromium oxide green are placed on either side of the bisecting lines and along the edges of the permanent green light area of the back of the frog's head rock.

Painting the Frog

Materials. The basic equipment described under "Paints and Brushes" is used for painting the frog. You will need #000, #1 and #10 red sable brushes, gesso, cadmium yellow medium, permanent green light, chromium oxide green, cadmium red light, black, and white acrylics.

Procedure. Using the #10 brush, gesso the body and head rocks. Though some gesso may be accidentally brushed onto feet and eyes, you need cover only head and body rocks completely.

Again using a #10 brush, apply two base coats of lime or chartreuse (permanent green light + cadmium yellow medium + white) to the body and head. Feet and eyes need not be painted this color.

Next, the feet should be painted permanent green light, using a #1 or #000 brush to first edge the tops, then moving to the sides and bottoms. Two coats will be needed here as well.

The design on the back, basically a spade, is outlined in permanent green light. Start at the back of the neck, and move down, out and back, returning to the center at the bottom, approximately where a tail would be placed. Repeat for the other side and fill in the outline with permanent green light.

Now use a #1 brush to apply permanent green light to the head by starting at a point or peak at the back, moving around one side to form a dipping curve, then around to the front to form a slightly dipping curve, as seen in the three sketches here.

Paint all the head area above this line, including eyes, permanent green light. Though the front part of the eyes will later be painted white, painting only the rear portion of the eyes at this time is false economy of time and paint, since painting only half the eye rock leaves a hard-to-cover line where green paint ends. Two coats of permanent green light will be needed for head and back designs.

Now, using a #000 brush, draw a lime or chartreuse line from the top of the spade all the way onto the chartreuse base coat at the point of the spade. You will need a second coat for this line, but this should be applied later, since it can serve to cover marks of chromium oxide green that may get onto the original line.

Repeat this chartreuse line procedure on the head rock, this time starting the line midway between the two eye rocks and ending it just as it enters the peak at the lower back portion of the head. Again, you will need to apply the second coat later, since that coat will cover any marks of chromium oxide green which may get onto the original line.

Using a #000 brush and chromium oxide green, draw a series of half ovals that seem to be bisected by the chartreuse line of the head. Most head rocks have ample room for three ovals, but small ones may have room for only two. Continue the head design by painting approximately three half ovals on the right side of the head, letting the flat side of the half ovals touch the lower edge of the permanent green light section of the head as shown in the photograph. Repeat for the left side.

The markings along the chartreuse line that bisects the spade on the frog's back are like those along the chartreuse line bisecting his head. When you have outlined and filled in the series of half ovals along the chartreuse line on the head, proceed with the markings along the line through the spade design. These marking are less regular in shape and spacing than those on the head.

Place a chromium oxide green moundlike marking at the top of each side of the spade; then paint two more of these mounds along

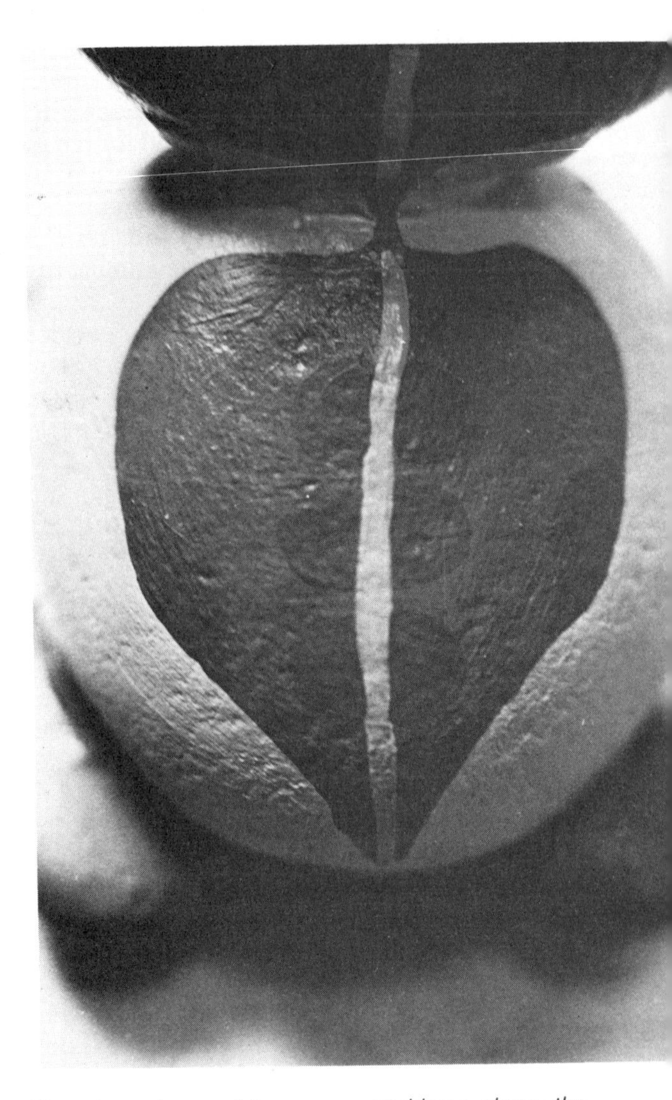

The chromium oxide green markings along the edges of the spade are less regular than those of the head rock.

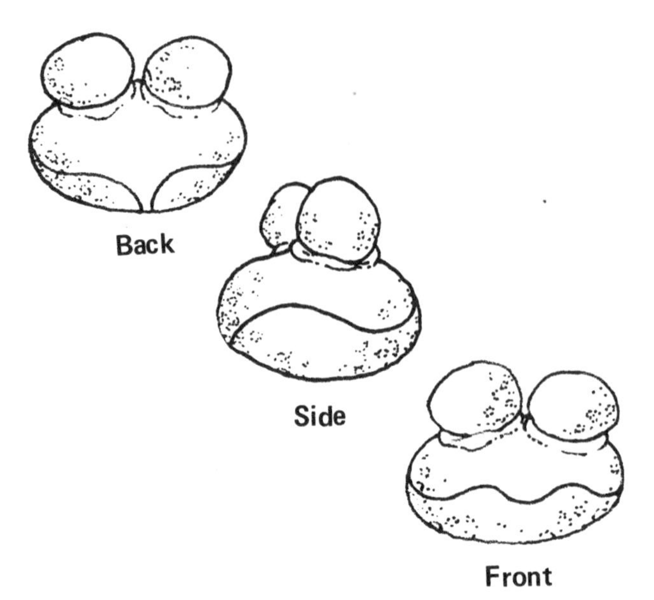

the lower portion of each side of the spade. Start each mound by drawing a chromium oxide green line of the appropriate length along the inside edge of the spade. Then draw a slight hump or half circle whose edges are at each end of this line and fill in the hump with chromium oxide green.

Use the #000 to outline three elongated "V"'s on each foot, and the same brush to apply a second coat of chartreuse or lime to the lines bisecting the head and back of the frog. When the "V"'s of the toes have dried, complete the feet by applying a chartreuse dot to the point of each "V."

Use the #000 brush and permanent green

light to outline three circles on the frog's right side, almost directly to the right of the widest portion of the spade design on his back. The largest circle should be nearest the shoulder area; the other two, behind this first one. Repeat this procedure for the frog's left side, then use a #000 brush to place an off-centered chromium oxide green dot in each circle.

Begin painting the frog's facial features by using a #1 brush to apply white paint to the front third of each eye rock. The eyeballs usually require three or more coats of paint.

When the final coat of white has dried, use a #000 brush to outline two black pupils, quite crossed, so that the frog will appear to be looking down at the ladybug on his nose.

Using a #000 brush and black acrylic, draw two up-curved eye wrinkles on the flat surface of the head rock just forward of each eye. Following the line where the two greens meet, outline a mouth whose edges curve up onto the permanent green light portion of the head. Add smile lines in the corners and make a licking tongue, if you like. Two U-shaped nose marks, spaced as shown in the photo, complete the facial features, except for the two white dots which add a sparkle to the frog's eyes. Since the eyes are crossed and looking noseward, superimpose the white dots on the lower inside portion of the black pupils.

The small, oval rock that forms the ladybug perched on the frog's nose is placed on a piece of masking tape for painting. Being careful to get under the edges of the rock, use a #1 brush to apply several coats of cadmium red light. Then use a #000 brush to draw a black curved line, thus outlining the head portion of the ladybug. The head area is then painted black, and random black spots are superimposed on the cadmium red portion of the bug's body. For even spacing of the spots, form a row of spots around the outer edge of the body, then fill in spots in the remaining space.

Two white eye dots are placed on the black face, and two black pupils are superimposed on these dots. After allowing adequate drying time for the finished bug, use a toothpick to place a dab of glue on her underside and press her gently, but firmly, into place on the frog's nose. Try to position her so that both her eyes peer into one of the frog's eyes, while both of his eyes cross in their effort to look down at her.

Your frog and ladybug are ready to be checked for blemishes, retouched, and sprayed with a plastic fixative. Be sure to observe the directions and safety precautions given under "Spraying the Figures."

Your finished frog is ready to add interest to an end table, give a bright touch to a terrarium, or delight a favorite nephew or niece. Whatever his size or function, he's sure to become an eye-catching addition to home or garden.

Elephant

Instructions for three types of elephants are given in this section. The plain gray elephant has a tiny white mouse climbing along his trunk. The pink elephant's bloodshot eyes and party hat make him a favorite New Year's gift. The natural-rock, circus elephant wears a decorative headpiece and blanket of red and gold. All three seem equally popular with the public. Master one or all of the following designs, then try variations of your own.

Choosing the Rocks

Ten rocks are required for each of the three elephant models. Since the main rocks of the circus elephant are left in their natural state, match the head, body, trunk, ears, and tail as to texture and color. Remember that spraying on fixative deepens the colors of unpainted rocks and often brings out subtle variations not apparent before spray is applied. Since wetting the rocks gives the effect of the spray temporarily, compare rocks while wet to achieve the best match.

A fat, oval body rock is preferable, though a relatively thin oval can be used. The head rock, basically a turtle rock, should not be too flat. The flatter side will be glued to the body, with the fuller side forming the face.

Choose four oval or round foot rocks of similar size and thickness. Since even the circus elephant's feet may be painted, you need not worry about matching colors and textures. Choose a short, elongated tail rock.

Ears with one curved side and one relatively straight side are best, since the straight edge can be more easily glued to the head and body rocks. Ideally, the straight inner portion should be a bit thinner than the curved outer portion of the ear rock.

The trunk rock should be a small, nearly cylindrical rock with one end flatter and wider than the other. Try placing several trunk rocks against the face, letting the flatter, wider end be the base of the trunk and the tapered, narrower end the trunk's top. The tip of the trunk should point upward, in trumpeting position. Be sure to get a trunk that's large enough for your particular elephant, yet leaves ample room for a large eye on each side. If you're making a gray elephant that will have a mouse on his trunk, you may wish to pick a less cylindrical trunk rock whose flatter surface will make gluing the mouse on simpler.

The one-rock mouse is made of a small oval rock, larger at one end than the other. Ideally, the mouse should have a flat underside.

The pink elephant's party hat is made of three rocks of graduated sizes. A flat, round rock is needed for the hat's base. A smaller rock of the same shape and thickness will be placed on the bottom one. A small, round rock will be needed for the ball at the top of the hat.

The Gluing

Materials. The rough working surface, glue, glue sticks, and props described in the turtle section are also used for assembling the elephant. In addition, you will need two cylindrical rocks for holding the ears in place during the drying process. The length of these rocks depends on the finished elephant's height.

Procedure—Gray Elephant. Place the four foot rocks together so that the two rear ones point outward slightly. The two front ones seem to provide a sturdier base and better balance when pointed straight ahead. Try placing the body rock onto the four foot rocks. Since the elephant's head will be slightly cantilevered, try balancing it against the body to be sure its weight won't cause the finished elephant to tip forward on its trunk. If tipping seems likely, move the two front feet farther forward.

Then press down gently on the body rock and jiggle each foot rock to be sure that each foot meets both body and table surfaces. Rearrange the foot rocks to achieve the best combination. When satisfied with the fit, place a generous blob of glue on each foot rock and press the body rock firmly, but gently, into place.

Get chips and wood scraps ready for propping. Then try positioning the head rock so that the flatter side of the rock rests against the body rock. Apply a blob of glue to the head rock, press it into place, and prop it with wood scraps and chips.

If you aren't in a hurry to complete your elephant, you should let the rocks dry overnight before gluing on ears, tail, and trunk. If you are pressed for time, go on to the next gluing operation now, being careful to avoid disturbing the rocks you have just glued.

Since the thinner portion of each ear should be placed between the elephant's head and body, apply a generous amount of glue to both front and back edges of the rock so that it will be joined to both head and body surfaces. Now, slip the ear into place, applying firm, but gentle, pressure. Place chips and wood scraps beneath the ear and lean a prop rock against the back of the ear, near the glued edge. This will help to hold the ear in place and will also give it the desired flapped-forward angle. Repeat this procedure for the other ear, being careful to have the top of both ears at approximately the same height.

The trunk should be positioned so that the elephant appears to be holding it upward, almost as if trumpeting. Place the rock's flatter edge against the head rock, leaving the more rounded edge up. The flatter, wider end of the trunk rock, the base of the trunk, should be placed against the head rock, leaving enough space for the mouth at the bottom of the head rock. The trunk should be in an almost perpendicular position, so there will be room for a large eye on each side of it.

When satisfied with the trunk's position, apply a liberal dab of thick glue along the entire length of the trunk's flatter side and press the trunk into place. If your glue is thick enough, no props will be needed, but use props if you think there is any danger of the trunk's sliding out of position. Use your index

Make a pink elephant with blood-shot eyes and party hat, a grey elephant with a white mouse on his trunk, or a natural rock circus elephant with a decorative headpiece and blanket.

Trunk, tail, and ears are propped for drying. Note the prop rocks which are leaned against the backs of the ears.

finger to remove excess glue, since this is easier than trimming dried glue later with a razor blade.

The short *tail* rock should be placed at the end of the body rock, pointing downward. Apply a liberal dab of thick glue to the tail rock and press it into place. Prop if the rock's weight seems likely to make it slide out of place.

The one-rock mouse, which requires no preliminary gluing, will be glued onto the trunk after both elephant and mouse have been painted.

If you're painting a pink elephant, you should glue his three-rock party hat together at this time so that it will be ready to paint when you are ready for it. Apply glue to the bottom of the middle-sized rock, center it on the largest rock, and press it into place. Then apply glue to the bottom of the smallest rock, center that rock on the middle-sized one, and press it gently, but firmly, into place. The hat and the elephant will both be painted before the hat is glued onto the elephant's head.

Before beginning to trim and paint, allow the elephant to dry for several days, or until the white glue turns clear.

Painting

Materials. For all three elephant designs you will need the basic equipment described early in the book, including black and white acrylics and #10, #1, and #000 red sable brushes. The accompanying chart shows the additional acrylics needed for each of the designs. The pink elephant also requires the use of gesso undercoating agent.

COLOR	ELEPHANT
Pthalocyanine blue + white = light blue	gray, circus
Yellow oxide	circus
Cadmium red light	circus
Crimson red	pink
Napthol ITR crimson + white = party pink	gray, pink

Procedure—Gray Elephant. Since light gray elephants seem to have more appeal than darker ones, be sure to use enough white when mixing the basic gray shade. Mix enough paint for good coverage, plus touch-ups later. Storing the paint in a tightly covered plastic container will keep it from drying out too quickly.

Using a #10 brush to achieve a smooth finish, cover the entire elephant with gray acrylic. Start with the feet, let them dry, then paint the rest of him, being careful to cover all the jointed areas and the hard-to-reach spots around the edges of the trunk, ears, tail, and feet. Use a second coat, if necessary.

The facial features of the gray elephant are painted next. Use a #000 brush and black paint to draw on two eyebrows, the outlines of two large oval eyes, two curly lashes at the top, outer edges of the eyes, two wrinkle lines beneath each eye, and a small, curving mouth with two laugh lines at each corner.

Then use a #000 brush to outline the opening at the trunk's tip, following the

Your gray elephant is ready to be checked for stray specks of paint or other blemishes, re-touched, and given a protective coating of fixative.

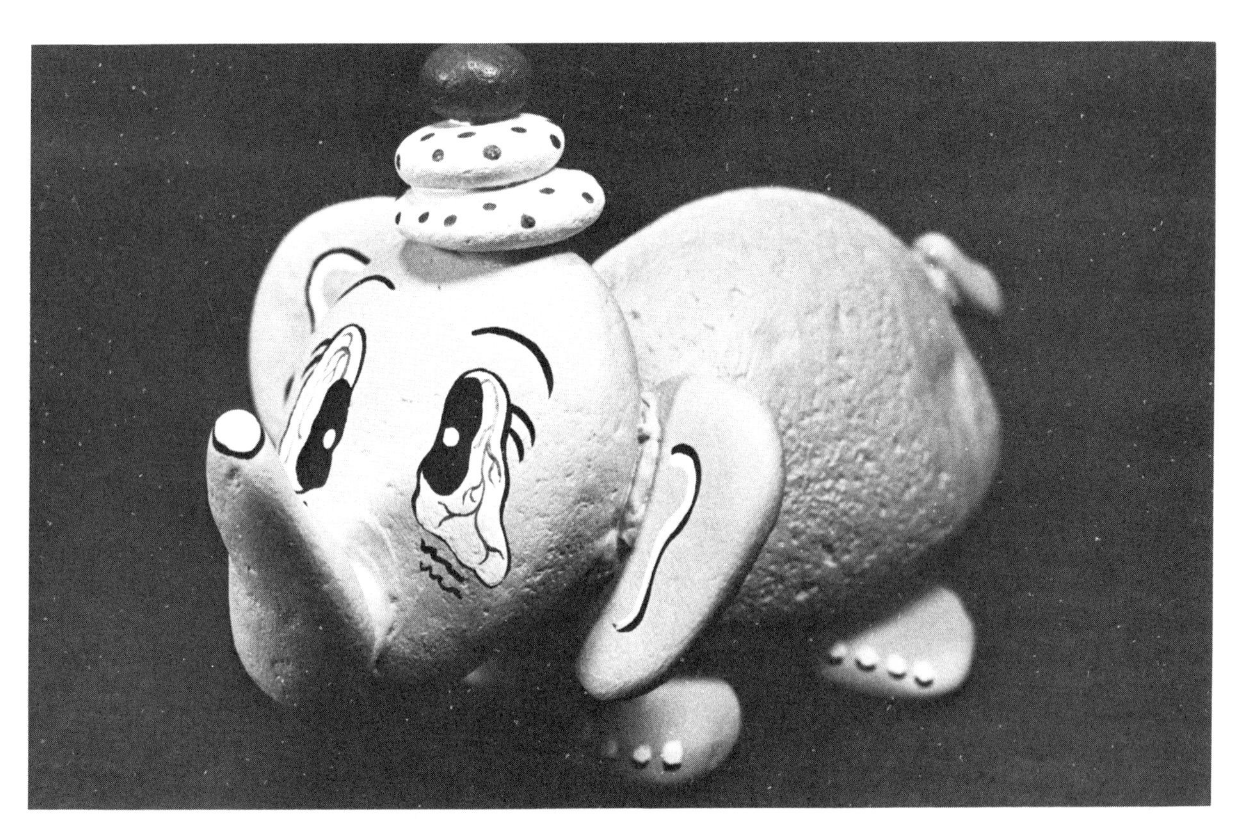

Since crimson red tends to run if sprayed too heavily, apply a very light coating of fixative to the pink elephant's eyes, tongue, and party hat.

Note that the facial features of the circus elephant are essentially the same as those of the grey elephant.

general shape of the end of the rock and adding a small tail pointing downward on one side so the outline resembles a tadpole. Use the #000 brush to outline a vague "3" in each ear, creating the illusion of an opening.

Now use the #1 or #000 to fill in the eyes with white, applying two to three coats. While the first eye coat dries, use the brush to make four white toenail dots on each foot and to outline the inner edges of each ear opening in white.

When the final coat of white on the elephant's eyes has dried, use the #000 brush to outline two black pupils. Place these pupils near the lower inside corners of the eyeballs, so that the eyes appear crossed and looking downward. While the pupils are drying, outline the lower half of each toenail in black.

Using the #000 brush and light blue acrylic (pthalocynanine blue + white), outline the black pupils wherever the pupils don't touch the inner edges of the eyes. Starting at the middle point of the area to be outlined, apply lessening brush pressure as you move down and around so that the outline is thinner around the lower portion of the eye. Then go back to the midpoint and outline the eye's upper portion. Repeat for the other eye.

Use the #000 to superimpose a white dot on the black pupil. Since the elephant is looking down at the mouse on his trunk, the dot should be in the lower inside portion of each pupil.

The mouse that the elephant is gazing at should be painted before he is glued into place. Place the mouse rock, flatter side down, on a piece of masking tape. Now use the #1 brush to apply several coats of white paint, allowing adequate drying time between each coat. The smaller end should be the mouse's head. Create his facial features by using a #000 brush and *thin* black acrylic to make two black eye dots, two thin brows, a U-shaped nose, an up-curved mouth, and two inverted "U" ears. When the black paint has dried, fill in each ear outline with soft party pink (napthol ITR crimson + white).

When the mouse has thoroughly dried, remove him from the masking tape and try positioning him on the trunk so that there will be room to paint his white tail directly on the trunk. Placing him against a relatively flat section of the trunk is essential to ensure a firm hold. When satisfied with the position, use a toothpick to apply a generous dab of *thick* glue to the mouse's underside. Then press him firmly into place. Since the mouse is relatively light, no props should be needed. In fact, if props do prove necessary, you'll have to leave the mouse propped in place until the glue sets well enough to allow you to remove the props before you can paint his tail on the trunk. Using thick glue (see the section "Gluing the Rocks" in the turtle section) avoids risking this delay.

To make the mouse's tail, use a #000 brush and white paint. Starting far enough under the mouse's rear edge to be sure the tail seems to be attached to the mouse, apply relatively firm pressure as you form the base of the tail, lessening the pressure as you thin the tail toward its tip.

Your gray elephant is now ready to be checked for blemishes or stray specks of paint, retouched where necessary, and sprayed with a satin-finish plastic fixative. Reread the directions under "Spraying the Figures," and be sure to observe all safety precautions.

Procedure—Pink Elephant. The pink elephant, obviously the victim of too much partying, is first given a coating of gesso. When the gesso has dried, apply two coats of party pink (napthol ITR crimson + white) to the entire elephant. Using a #10 brush to apply both the gesso and the party pink acrylic will help to ensure a smoother finish.

The wavy, irregular outlines of the pink elephant's bloodshot eyes reveal his raveled state. No set pattern is called for, but making the outline stand higher on the nose side and droop or melt down the outside achieves the desired effect. Add two drooping lashes to each eye and two raveled wrinkle lines. His brows are simple arches, like those of the gray elephant.

The nose is a simple ring which follows the contour of the trunk rock and, like the gray elephant's, ends in a small downward line or "tail." Give the illusion of ear openings by outlining a vague "3" in each ear. Still with the

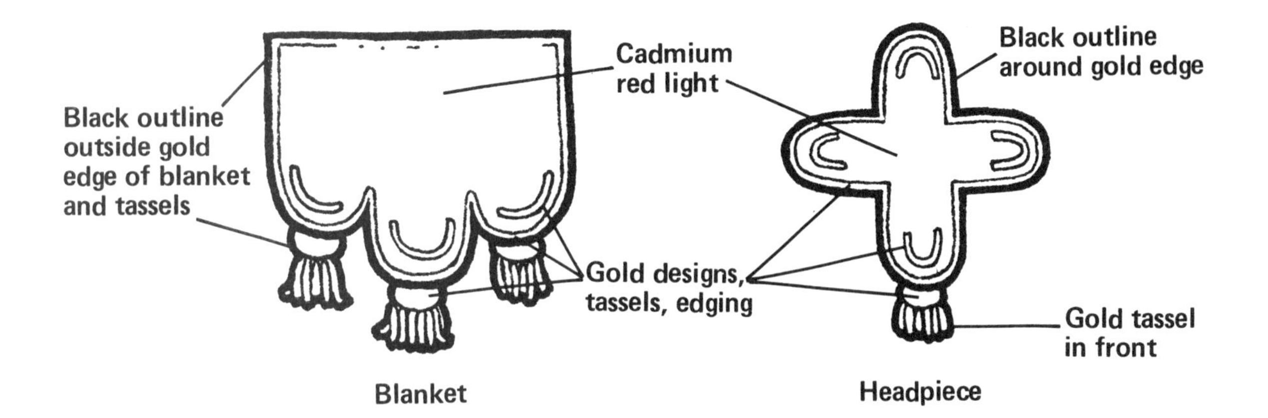

black, make a drooping, unhappy mouth with a tired tongue hanging out. Then apply at least two coats of crimson red to the tongue.

Now, with white, fill in the eyes (two to three coats), outline the inside of each ear opening, and paint four nail dots on each foot. Now is a good time to apply two coats of white to the bottom sections of the party hat. Hold the hat by the top rock and be sure to cover the hat's underside well.

When the whites of the eyes have dried, use the #000 brush to outline two black pupils with wobbly edges. For best results, make imperfect ovals and paint the pupil of one eye near its top edge and the pupil of the other near its bottom edge. Then outline the lower half of each toenail in black.

The crimson red lines in the elephant's bleary eyes should be painted now. The finished eye lines should look like the root system of a plant. Use the #000 brush to draw the main vein first. This first line should almost bisect the eyeball and should branch into a fork at its lower end. Add a few smaller vein lines branching off and down from the main vein. A few of these may also branch into tiny forks. Random spacing works best, and don't overcrowd the white area. The bloodshot eyes do not need to match—after all, whose would?

Then, since even a pink elephant has a bit of spunk left, place a tiny white dot in each pupil.

The elephant's party hat should be finished at this time. If you've already painted the two bottom sections in white, hold the hat by the top rock and use the #000 brush to apply randomly spaced crimson red dots to the white area. Since you need not dot the white underside of the bottom rock, you may set the hat down while the dots dry. When the dots have dried, paint the top section of the hat crimson red.

When the hat has dried, try placing it on the elephant's head at an angle that suggests the condition of its wearer. Be sure the area of the head has a flat enough surface to ensure a good hold for the hat. Then apply a generous dab of thick glue to the underside of the hat's largest rock and press the hat into place. If your glue is a bit thin, you may need to hold the hat in place for a few minutes until you feel it is no longer in danger of sliding. If the hat still seems likely to slide, prop poker chips between the elephant's back and the edge of the hat.

Check the entire elephant for stray paint specks or blemishes, retouch where necessary, and spray on a satin-sheen plastic fixative. Since crimson red tends to run if sprayed too heavily, apply a very light coating of fixative to the eyes, tongue, and party hat.

Procedure—Circus Elephant. Though the circus elephant's body may be painted gray before his decorative blanket and headgear are added, an elephant of natural rock is especially attractive. If you haven't managed to match the colors of the foot rocks, you should use a #1 or #000 brush to paint the four feet gray, in a shade that approximates the natural gray of the elephant's body.

When beginning the elephant's blanket and headpiece, remember that working on natural rocks means you will not be able to paint over your goofs. Be especially careful when making the working outline of the decorations.

Use a #1 brush and cadmium red light to outline a blanket on the elephant's back. The drawing here shows the basic outline. Fill in the blanket with cadmium red, using a #10 brush to achieve a smooth finish if you're covering a very large area.

Then use a #000 brush to outline the blanket's outer edge in gold (yellow oxide) and make the gold inner markings, balls, and tassels. When this has dried, outline the gold balls, tassels, and outer edge of the blanket in *thin* black acrylic.

Using a #000 brush and cadmium red light, outline the cloverlike headpiece. Let the front section droop down onto the elephant's forehead and the rear section hang down the back of his head. Fill in the headpiece with cadmium red light, add a single gold tassel above the forehead, outline the headpiece in gold, and make gold interior markings. Then outline the gold outer edge in *thin* black acrylic.

The circus elephant's facial features are the same as those of the gray elephant. Again, remember that you should be especially careful to avoid making serious mistakes, since you want to preserve the natural rock finish and avoid having to apply a gray base coat to cover your painting errors.

When the facial features are completed, check for blemishes or stray specks of paint, do all necessary retouching, and apply a protective satin-sheen coating. Since natural rocks take on an undesirable plastic look if sprayed too heavily, apply only a single coat of fixative.

Whether you've made a gray elephant with a white mouse on his trunk, a pink elephant whose bleary eyes show the effects of too much partying, or a circus elephant whose red and gold trappings highlight the colors and textures of natural rock, your elephant is sure to bring favorable comments from observers of all ages.

Bear

Modeling paste gives a natural, furry look to one of the more advanced animals in the "Daystone" menagerie, the lazy bear. With a little patience and careful attention to the directions which follow, a rockcrafter who has learned the basics by trying simpler insects and animals should be able to create an attractive, winsome bear.

Choosing the Rocks

Nine rocks are needed for a lazy bear, plus one rock or log for the bear to lean against. The head rock may be round, but oval rocks slightly pointed at one end make better bear heads, since the pointed portion seems more like a bear's muzzle.

A rounded rock, slightly flat on one edge and about twice as thick as a turtle's body makes a suitable body rock, since the lazy bear is lying on his back with his fat tummy in full view. Four paw rocks are needed, and the two that form the front paws may be slightly smaller and more rounded than the two for the hind paws. The hind paws should be slightly elongated, similar in shape to a very wide human foot.

The two small ear rocks should be approximately equal in size but may be round, oval, or even slightly irregular in shape, since modeling paste will cover them entirely. The nose rock should be about the same size as the ear rocks, but it must be almost perfectly round, since no modeling paste will be applied to it.

The log against which the bear leans may be part of a small, freshly cut branch or a scrap of weathered branch or log. If you prefer that lazy bear lie against a rock, the rock may be painted or left in its natural state, but for best results it should probably be log-shaped so that it fits snugly into the space between head and neck.

The Gluing

Materials. The rough working surface, glue, glue stick, and props described in the turtle section are also used for assembling the bear. In addition, you will need modeling paste shaded with burnt sienna, a palette

From his lounging position, this lazy bear takes a bright-eyed look at the world.

knife, and a rat-tailed comb for making bear hair or fur. You will need to work near the sink or with a deep jar or bowl of water in order to clean the comb frequently, and a paint cloth or paper towel will be needed to wipe the damp comb.

Procedure—Rocks. Set the body rock on its flat side and try placing the oval head rock so that the most pointed end (chin or muzzle end) lies on the bear's chest. Then, with props ready, apply a generous dab of glue to the head where it meets the bear's body. Now use wood scraps and chips to prop the head at this angle.

Very thick glue is needed for ears and nose, for no props are used to keep these in place during the drying time. Thinking of the top portion of the bear's head as the top half of a clock face, try positioning the ear rocks at approximately 10:30 and 1:30. Then place a generous dab of glue on one ear and press the ear firmly into place. Repeat this procedure for the second ear.

The nose is placed near the very end of the muzzle (most pointed area of the face). No space need be left at the muzzle's tip for the mouth, since the mouth line will be painted beneath the nose and on the underside of the pointed portion of the head rock. Excess glue can be trimmed away later, so be sure to use enough to hold the nose securely in place.

When the nose has been glued, all preliminary gluing has been completed and the bear should be allowed to dry for several days or until the white tacky glue is nearly clear before modeling paste is applied. Paw rocks will be glued on later, as explained later in the section.

When the bear has thoroughly dried, use a single-edged razor blade to trim excess glue from around his nose and to trim any large amount of glue that may have run down his back. All other glued areas will be covered with modeling paste and need not be trimmed.

Procedure—The Fur. Modeling paste is used to make the bear's fur. When deciding on a suitable modeling paste, remember the tip given under "Modeling Paste" in the first part, and consider using a half-and-half mixture of two brands.

Since chipping of paint could expose this paste base later, be sure to add burnt sienna acrylic paint to the modeling-paste mixture. An already colored paste base makes the painting job easier, too. For a 4- to 6-inch bear, use about 4 tablespoons of modeling paste, adding acrylic paint until the mixture approaches burnt sienna in tone.

Using a palette knife, start applying the paste to the head rock just behind the top edge of the nose. Work upward to the top of the head rock and then around to the right, leaving a space for the white area that will surround the eye. Making sure to leave the same amount of space for the other eye, repeat this procedure on the other side of his face.

Next, spread the paste down and around

the right side of the face, then the left, leaving a space for the eyes, as shown in the photograph. Work these sideburn areas down to the very base of the head rock, covering all glued areas there. Cover the back of the head and the ears with modeling paste; then cover the front of the ears with the paste.

Now the bear's fur must be combed and styled, using a rat-tailed comb which has been broken off at the top end so that the teeth extend to the very tip of the comb.

Using the teeth at the comb's tip end and enough pressure to leave lines but not expose the rock's surface, comb upward and outward from the nose. Wash the comb frequently, using cold running water or dipping the comb in a jar of water, since excessive build-up of modeling paste prevents formation of satisfactory hairlike lines. Be sure to wipe excess water from the teeth with a paper towel or cloth before resuming the combing of modeling paste, since too much water should not be mixed into the paste.

When the middle strip of paste has been combed upward to the top of the head rock, comb the sideburn areas upward and outward to the ears. Then comb the ears, bringing them to a point at the top. Start at the base of the neck on the back of the head rock and comb upward and outward, finally working front and back combing lines together at the top and sides of the head rock.

Finally, do a bit of styling, working to point the ears in a natural manner and to comb out bits of paste so that the sideburn areas seem to be particularly bushy. Extra modeling paste may be needed to achieve the desired look in the fringed areas of the sides of the face.

When the head has been modeled and combed, begin work on the body, remembering to leave a large, bare oval for the tummy area and the center portion of the back free of modeling paste.

Hold the bear so that your thumb is on his tummy area and your fingers rest on his center back. Then, using the palette knife, place modeling paste at the top of his back at the neckline, working the paste all the way around the right side of his back to the tail area. Add more paste as needed, creating a similar border around the left side of the bear's back. Starting at each shoulder in turn, bring paste around to the tail area on the bear's tummy side. As you work in the areas where head and body meet, be sure not to leave him hairless around the back neck area. When the paste covers the designated area, use the palette knife to smooth the paste, using strokes similar to those used in frosting cakes or cupcakes—the fur's fudge color may even make you hungry!

Most of the modeling paste on the body rock will be combed off, since more pressure is used for body combing than for head combing. Combing downward from bare tummy area around to backside, exert enough pressure to cause the teeth to expose the rock's surface. Since such heavy pressure causes rapid paste build-up on the comb, be sure to wash and wipe the comb frequently enough to ensure formation of a clear, clean set of lines.

When combing has been completed, allow the bear to dry for approximately three hours, propping with a chip if necessary to avoid letting any of the rocks rest on an area covered with modeling paste. Overnight drying is even better, since you want to avoid disturbing the comb lines when you begin to paint on the facial features.

At this point you can save time later by checking the unpasted areas of the bear's face and stomach for rough, pitted places that might cause painting problems. Any severely pitted areas should be filled in with white modeling paste before paint is applied. By doing this patching now, the white paste can be drying while the furry area dries.

Allow the modeling paste to dry thoroughly. If small cracks appear after the paste has dried, put a small amount of modeling paste on your index finger and fill in the cracks. Be especially careful to spot and repair cracks on the ears, since the paste is probably thicker there and hence more likely to crack.

Painting

Materials. Burnt sienna, pthalocyanine blue, black, and white acrylics and #10, #1, and #000 red sable brushes are needed for the bear. Refer to the "Paints and Brushes" section near the beginning of the book for other

Work upward to the top of the head, then around to the right, leaving a space for the white area that will surround the left eye.

A blue outline is painted around the outer edge of the black pupil.

basic equipment needed for painting rockcrafted items.

Procedure. Using a #1 brush outline and fill in all the bear's bare spots on his head and stomach with white, being sure to cover right up to the edge of the modeling paste. Then use a #10 brush to smooth out the large areas of white. After the first coat is dry, add a second one, and a third, if necessary.

Then, with a #10 brush and burnt sienna, paint the furry areas of the bear's body, starting with the head and edge of stomach area. Turn the bear over, nose down, and allow three to five minutes of drying time. Then paint his sides and back, including the smooth, bare area of the back which has no modeling paste on it.

When the brown paint has dried, retouch any spots where brown paint may have been smeared on the white area.

The bear's facial features are then outlined. Begin by using a #000 brush and black paint to draw on eyebrows. Be sure both brows are about the same distance from the brown, furry region of the head.

At this point, you may choose to create a lazy, but wide-eyed bear or a soundly sleeping one. For the wide-eyed one, the outline is made by first drawing the double curve which forms the bottom of the eye. Then add an inverted "u" over it and two lashes, followed by two wrinkle lines below.

The sleeping bear's eyes are very easy to fashion, since each eye is really a miniature smile line with slightly curly lashes drawn below. Use a #000 brush and black acrylic for these eyes, and remember to place them where the *bottom* line of an open eye would be placed.

Still using the #000 brush, paint the bear's nose black. Then draw his mouth line, a deepened, U-shaped version of a smile, and add corner lines to the mouth. Finally, use the #000 brush and black acrylic to draw on a belly button like the one in the photograph of the finished bear.

If you're making a wide-eyed bear, now is the time to superimpose the pupil on the white eyeball, remembering to make the eyes slightly crossed and looking up at you. The bear's pupils may be left totally black, but a blue outline adds personality to this lazy fellow. Mix pthalocyanine blue and white for this eye color. Notice that the blue outline is painted only along the outer and not along the bottom edge of each pupil. A white dot adds a glint to each bright blue eye.

The bear's paws are painted before they are glued to his body. Place both pairs of paws on a piece of masking tape and use the #10 brush and burnt sienna to paint each paw, being sure to get the brush as far under the edges as possible, since these edges will show when the paw is glued onto the body. The tape will usually hold the center portion of each paw, even if you paint under all edges.

When the paws have dried completely, place four dots for claws on each front paw, remembering that the front paws are the smaller of the two pairs. Claws are shown for forepaws because the bear's position indicates that the tops of these paws would be exposed to view.

Since the bottoms of the hind feet are exposed, outline the center part of each foot in white, roughly forming the shape of a human foot, minus the toes. Two or more coats of white will be necessary. When the last coat has dried, make the crease lines in each foot as seen in the photo of the finished bear.

Be sure the paws are thoroughly dry to avoid smearing brown paint on the white portion of the stomach when you experiment with the various positions before gluing on the paws. The front paws should be placed so that the claws are at the bottom of each paw and so that the paws seem to be relaxed and limp—as they would probably be if the bear were lying on his back. Hind paws are glued so that the eyebrow-shaped curve of the crease line is at the top of each foot.

When the best positioning has been determined, place a generous dab of glue on each paw and press firmly into place. Use enough glue to ensure a good hold, but avoid an excessive amount that might leave unsightly glue smears on the finished body rock.

The log or rock against which the bear is lying should now be rubbed against the back of the bear's head and body until scratch marks appear on the back of the head and body where the rock or log touches them. Place generous dabs of glue at these marks and then press the bear against his resting place, being careful not to disturb the freshly glued paws. Allow him to dry for several days or until the glue turns clear.

When the bear has dried, use a #000

brush and black paint to sign your name or initials on his underside, if you like. Then check the finished bear for scratches or stray flecks of paint. Do all retouching first, then spray on the plastic fixative, following directions and precautions given in the section "Spraying the Figures."

Your lazy bear is ready to greet the world, or your sleeping bear to doze his life away. Either way, you've completed a rockcraft item that will delight family and friends.

Owl

Rockcrafting owls the Daystone way requires time and patience but yields beautiful results—custom-made owls with a professional appearance. Learn the special antiquing operation whose browns, reds, and yellows produce a strikingly realistic owl. Or create a graduation owl, complete with mortarboard, school colors, monogram, and graduation date. Finally, if you're fortunate enough to find round head and body rocks with color and texture too beautiful to hide, add modeling-paste feathering in shades which complement the natural hues, but leave most of the body and face in their natural state.

All three versions of the owl make excellent graduation gifts, though the second type is obviously far more personalized. You'll be amazed at the number of people who'll exclaim, "I just love owls!", for owls are favorite collectors' items across the country.

Choose the variety best suited to your personal interest and proceed according to the directions given below. Prepainting steps vary so slightly that no subdivisions are made for the three types until the painting section.

Choosing the Rocks

The large, round body and head rocks needed for an owl are among the most difficult types to locate. Fortunately, these rocks need not be smooth. In fact, the owl's antiqued finish makes a rough, pitted surface highly desirable. A large head, in proportion to the body, can also be an asset.

If you plan to make variation three, the natural-rock owl, rock hunting will be considerably more difficult, for you will need to consider surface color and texture as well as shape. If you're fortunate enough to find a head and body rock that have black and white mottling, try the specific painting technique given in the painting section for the natural owl. Since this mottling is common in granite, you're more likely to find such rocks if you live in an area where granite abounds.

If you find beautiful rocks of other shades, read over the natural rock section, but improvise upon the technique by shading modeling paste and acrylics to complement the natural colors in your own rocks.

Eye rocks are the same size and shape for all three types of owls, and color is not a factor for antiqued or graduation owls. Choose eye rocks of dark gray or black for a natural owl made of granite. Choose rocks whose colors go well with whatever natural hues your particular rocks may contain. Since good owl eyes are relatively scarce, sort through the foot rocks you've collected and take out any round enough and flat enough to be used in this manner. These rocks should also be smooth enough to allow for ease in painting.

Owl ears are short, stubby rocks, much like those used for duck tails as described in a later section. Rocks of this shape which also have a flat surface make your gluing job much simpler. The short ends broken from mushroom stems (see the mushroom section) make especially good owl ears. Graduation owls don't require ear rocks, since the mortarboard won't fit over ears.

Ideally, the owl's beak should be a small, vaguely conical rock. The beak will be turned point downward when glued to the head rock.

Two flat, oblong rocks are needed for feet, and two medium-sized foot rocks serve as wings. The wings look best if they seem too short and stubby for actual flight.

The Gluing

Two separate gluing sessions are necessary when making an owl, and adequate drying time must be allowed between these sessions.

Materials. The rough working surface, glue, glue sticks, and props described in the turtle section are also used for assembling the owl. In addition, molding the owl's feathers requires properly shaded modeling paste, a palette knife, a jar of water, and a cloth or paper towel.

Notice how props are used to fill in the space between head rock and drying frame. The crisscrossed rubber bands hold the rocks in place during the drying period.

Gluing the owl is greatly simplified by the construction of a drying frame. Two 7″ × 7″ × ¾″ pieces of wood or plywood, six or seven finishing nails, and two ¼-inch rubber bands are needed for this frame.

Use two or three finishing nails to join the two pieces of wood at right angles as shown in the photo. Then hammer two nails into the top edge of the upright piece about one inch from each end. Hammer two more nails into the outer edge of the bottom piece of frame about one inch from each end. Hammer these nails in just far enough to ensure a firm hold but leave at least ½-inch of the nails exposed. The rubber bands will be crisscrossed from nail to nail to hold the owl rocks in place during the drying process.

Procedure—Rocks. Begin the first gluing session by placing two foot rocks side by side on the bottom board of the drying frame. Try balancing the body rock on the feet, remembering to turn the rock in a manner that will produce a fat, squatty owl rather than a tall, skinny, "pop bottle" one.

Now, press down on the body while jiggling the feet to be sure the body rock makes firm contact with both feet. Set the head rock on to be sure proportion of head to body is satisfactory. If the head rock is more oval than round, make the shorter sides of the oval the right and left sides of the head.

Apply a liberal dab of glue near the center of each foot and press the body rock firmly into place. Now, place the head rock right in the center of the body rock. If doing so means a space is left between head rock and the upright portion of the drying frame, fill in that space with wood scraps and/or poker chips. The head must be in contact with frame or props during the drying process.

Now, apply a liberal amount of glue to the center of the top of the body rock where body and head will meet, press the head rock into place, and hold it there while you crisscross the owl with two rubber bands as shown in the photo.

If you are careful to inch the rubberbands far enough inward where they cross the head rock, you'll have room on the head to glue on the ears during this session. But remember to omit the ears from any owl on which you intend to glue a mortarboard. Try placing the ears at about eleven o'clock and one o'clock. Then apply a liberal dab of *very* thick glue to each ear, press the ear into place, and hold it steady a moment or so before letting go.

If your glue is too thin, the ears will slide downward. You may be able to hold them in place until they no longer slip, if you are blessed with great amounts of patience. If this ear-holding session has upped your blood pressure and robbed you of the last ounce of that patience, refer to the glue-thickening process under "Gluing" in the turtle section, and prepare thicker glue for your next work session.

Allow the owl to dry on the frame for three days to one week or until the glue is almost

Support the wings with props during the drying period.

Apply the side of a palette knife filled with modeling paste to the center of the owl's forehead to make a single, elongated frond 3/8" to 1/2" above the beak. Add fronds on each side, framing the forehead in feathers.

clear. When drying time is over, you're ready for gluing session number two. Get wood scraps and poker chips ready for propping. Did you thicken that glue? You'll need it for these next steps.

Remove the owl from the drying frame. He won't budge? Then his feet are probably glued to the bottom board of the frame. If so, lay the frame flat so that the owl lies on his back. Then slip the flat edge of a chisel or broad screwdriver under one foot rock and tap the blunt end of screwdriver or chisel with a hammer until the foot rock is freed from the board. Use a single-edged razor blade to trim off any wood or excess glue that may still be stuck to the rocks.

When you have removed the owl from the frame, lay him on his back and try positioning the beak. The beak rock should be centered on the head and placed on its longest edge, producing a long, thin beak. When satisfied with placement of this rock, apply a liberal dab of glue to the edge that meets the head rock and press the beak gently but firmly into place. Hold it there a moment, then release it.

The eyes are glued next. Place the round, smooth eye rocks so that their inner edges touch the sides of the beak in much the same way that the two lenses of wire frame glasses are centered on each side of the nosepiece. When positioning seems optimum, apply a liberal dab of glue to each eye rock and press it into place.

The wings are glued last. Try placing the top of each wing on the shoulder area of the body rock, but be sure to leave enough space between wing and head to allow for working with the modeling paste. The wings will be angled outward slightly, following the outward curve of the top half of the owl's body rock. They should be just long enough to overhang the widest portion of the body rock just a bit.

When angle, overhang, and space between head and wings seem right, apply a liberal blob of glue to one wing, press it into place, and prop it with wood scraps and/or chips. Repeat for the other wing and allow the owl to dry on its back until the glue is nearly clear.

Procedure—Modeling Paste. When the owl has dried from his second gluing session, trim excess glue from around beak and eyes, being careful not to trim too close and lessen the bond. Then prepare the modeling paste that will be used to give the owl the ruffled-feathers look. Remember the half-and-half tip given under "Modeling Paste" in Part I.

For the antiqued owl, tint the modeling-paste mixture with enough burnt umber to produce a medium tan. The graduation owl requires modeling paste tinted with school color to be used predominantly during the painting process. Natural owls made from black and white granite rocks require black modeling paste, but match the paste to whatever complementary shade you've chosen, if you're using natural rocks of other hues.

Dip the palette knife into the tinted paste and apply the side of the paste-filled knife to the center of the forehead ⅜ to ½-inch above the beak, making a single, elongated frond. Add one frond on each side of the first, but a fraction higher on the forehead so that it will be the same distance from the eye. Then continue in this manner around one side of the forehead, framing it in feather fronds. Then frame the other side in like manner.

You will need to dip your palette knife into the jar of water frequently in order to avoid build-up of dry, flaking paste. Remember to wipe the knife dry with cloth or paper towel

This close-up shows the swirls along the "V" of the owl's back.

after each rinsing to avoid getting water in the paste.

Next, apply about a ¼-inch thickness of modeling paste to the ears and back of the head by starting at the center back of the neck and using the palette knife to apply the paste in a manner similar to that used when frosting a cake. WARNING: If you like chocolate icing, you'll probably be very hungry for the next few minutes.

Once this area has been covered, start at the base of the neck again and use the end of the palette knife, gentle pressure, and a slight, swirling motion, make a row of feathers along the base of the neck. Make a second row above, and a third and fourth, if needed, until you've reached the top of the head. Now work a single row from the top, front of the head onto the top row at the back of the head, leaving a ruffled appearance by swirling some paste loosely upward.

Starting at the back of the ears, style them in the same manner, using one or two short rows, depending on their size. Add extra paste whenever necessary. Make one or two rows of feathers on the front side of each ear, working the front and back top rows together to achieve a fringed or ruffled look.

Now apply more paste to one side of the face (from the ears to an area behind the eyes) by placing the palette knife flat edge down along the face, then pulling outward and upward, making a feathery fringe on that side of the face. Repeat for the other side, being careful to get the two sides as even as possible.

When this fringing is completed, fill in the area under the eyes and beak, but avoid getting modeling paste on the chest area. There's no need to try for swirls or rows in such close quarters, but do use your index finger to roughen up these chin feathers as much as possible.

Clean any excess modeling paste off chest, eyes, and beak to leave a smooth, even painting surface.

Begin body feathering by using the chocolate-frosting technique to apply a ½-inch layer of modeling paste to back and wings. Start by filling in the shoulders, then make a broad, poncholike "V" which extends from neckline about halfway down the back as shown in the photo.

Now make rows of feather swirls similar to but longer than those on the back of the owl's head. Begin row one at the point of the poncho and continue it up the right edge of the "V." Repeat this procedure on the "V"'s left side. Make a second V-shaped row of swirls in this manner, adding a third, if necessary, in the neck area. Check to be sure modeling paste for the body rock meets that of the head rock without any bare areas around neck and shoulders.

The wings should now be given a ¼-inch layer of modeling paste frosting. Check to be sure you have covered the top side of each wing all the way to the edges. Starting at the wing tip, use the same gentle pressure and slight, swirling motion to fashion three or four rows of feathers on each wing.

Allow the modeling paste to dry thoroughly. If small cracks appear after the paste has dried, put a small amount of modeling paste on your index finger and fill in the cracks. Be especially careful to spot and repair cracks on the ears, since the paste is probably thicker there and more likely to crack.

Since your modeling-paste feathering is finished and you must allow overnight drying time, why not make waiting easier by rewarding yourself with a batch of devil's food cupcakes—with chocolate icing, of course. No sense in further disappointing your tantalized tastebuds!

Painting the Owls

Follow the step-by-step painting instructions given below for the three variations on the basic owl design.

The Antiqued Owl. In addition to using the rockcrafting painting techniques you've already mastered, you will need to learn the antiquing operation which gives Daystone owls their distinctive appearance.

Burnt umber, red oxide, yellow oxide, chromium oxide green, white, and black acrylics; #000, #1, and #10 brushes; and gesso are the basic painting supplies needed for the antiqued owl. In addition to these basic items, the antiquing process requires the use of rubber gloves, a paper plate, old newspapers, and an optional small sponge.

The owl's base coat consists of gesso tinted with burnt umber to achieve a beige shade approximately the color of the modeling-paste feathering. This coat may be applied with a #10 brush or with a small sponge. Either method is messy, so cover your working area with old newspapers and don rubber gloves before starting to paint.

Hold the owl upside down by his feet and paint the bottom portions of body and head first. Still holding him by the feet, turn him right side up and move to the upper portions of body and head, using plenty of gesso and filling in all nooks and crannies of both modeling paste and rock surfaces. There's no need to gesso the feet, but no harm will be done if some gesso does get on them.

If you prefer a faster method, hold the owl by his feet and blot body, head, and wings with a sponge dipped in the gesso mixture. While somewhat faster, the sponge method tends to cause foamy, incomplete coverage, and some retouching with a brush will be required. Whether you use brush or sponge for initial coverage, give the tummy area a final smoothing with a brush to ensure a good painting surface.

Do *not* use this sponge technique in subsequent painting steps, since its tendency to cause bubbling and foaming is even more pronounced when the thin wash is applied and since bubbles in later coats cannot be hidden as well as those in this initial gesso coat.

When gesso coverage has been completed, double check to be sure no area above the feet has been missed. A good base is essential to the antiquing process. This beige coat must be thoroughly dry before the first wash is applied, since the thin wash will otherwise blend or bleed into the damp gesso, causing a running effect and destroying the graining effect toward which you are working. Allow six or more hours of drying time. Then check the areas around feet and neck to be sure no damp spots remain.

For step two, prepare a burnt umber and water wash of the consistency of water. This wash will have much the same effect as wood stain, since it dries to a darker shade where it has settled into hollows and pock marks. Again, wear rubber gloves and use old newspapers to cover your working surface.

Holding the owl's feet, use a #10 brush to stroke the wash lightly across all areas of head, wings, body, and eyes. Check to be sure shoulder and neck area have received adequate coverage. Do not try to paint the owl—merely "wash" him so that more of the liquid settles into the deep places, yet all areas have at least a light coating of the wash.

Adequate drying time is again essential to prevent bleeding or running of colors. Test the feet and neck areas after about four hours. Then touch up any areas where the wash failed to get into pitted or hollow spots. Recheck the backs and undersides of the wings and eyes, retouching if necessary. Allow these retouched spots to dry completely to avoid the risk of bleeding colors.

When you're sure the wash has thoroughly dried, squeeze a small amount of red oxide acrylic onto a paper plate. Dab the #10 brush lightly into this thick paint and strike the brush on the plate's surface until excess paint is used up and only a streaked effect remains.

When the brush holds only enough paint to produce this streaked coverage, start at the feathers of his forehead and brush red oxide over his entire head, body, and wings. Again, you are not painting the surface but merely tipping it. While the pitted areas retained the darkest layers of the thin, burnt umber wash, the raised areas will receive the greatest amount of red oxide. If you brush gently and avoid trying to fill in all the hollow areas, you will achieve a pleasing tricolor effect.

Though the outer surface of the eyes will later be painted white, you should avoid running the risk of leaving unpainted edges by painting the eyes lightly with red oxide.

Since this is mere tipping and not a heavy application of paint, the red oxide dries quickly. By the time you have washed and dried your brush and squeezed a blob of yellow oxide onto the paper plate, you should be able to begin tipping in that color.

Remember to apply the brush to the owl only after brushing excess paint out onto the surface of the paper plate. Use the same technique as before, lightly brushing the yellow oxide over the entire owl, including eyes but excluding feet and beak.

When the yellow oxide tipping has been completed, use a #1 or a #000 brush and burnt umber to paint the top edges of the feet. Then use a #10 to complete tops and bottoms of the feet, giving them a smooth, even finish. As you cover the feet, using a second coat, if needed, specks of red and yellow oxide should make clear the reason for delaying this painting step until now. Prop the owl, feet up, for a ten-minute drying time.

When the feet are dry enough for the owl to stand on them once more, paint his tummy area. Again using the paper plate as a palette, squeeze out individual dabs of red oxide, yellow oxide, and white. Now squeeze out a second dab of white and place a *small* dab of chromium oxide green beside this second dab. Mix the two colors to produce the pastel green needed for shading the lower portions of the tummy.

Painting the owl's chest and abdomen requires a combination of *shading and feather painting.* Look at a finished photo to see how the shaded area begins at the neck, just below the modeling-paste feathers of the chin area, and proceeds downward to approximately the point where the body rock starts to curve inward. There the shading ends in a curve which stretches across the lower abdomen and upward to the edges of the wings. The colors used, starting from the neck downward, are red oxide, yellow oxide, green, and white, wider bands of the first two, narrower of the second two.

An antiqued owl with feathers of modeling paste.

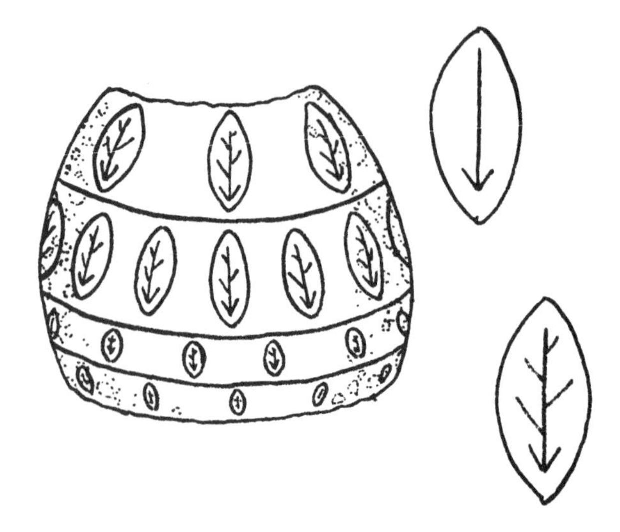

Beginning at the shoulders, paint the top third of the chest and abdomen area with red oxide. Use a #1 brush to get into close areas under the chin and between wing and head. Then use a #10 to give smoothness to the broad area across the chest. Cover the rock well; do *not* try for a streaked effect this time.

Using the #10 brush wherever possible, paint the middle third of this area with yellow oxide acrylic. When this band has been well covered, clean the #10 brush well, moisten it *slightly*, and blend the two color bands together where they meet, thus eliminating the striped polo-shirt look.

Use the #10 brush to apply pastel green to the next one-sixth of this area. When the green has been applied, clean the brush well, moisten it *slightly*, and blend the green line into the yellow by using firm, brisk strokes along the color seam.

The final band of color, a white one which covers the final sixth of the chest and abdomen area, is applied with a #1 brush. Be sure this line is curved upward toward the wings, not drawn straight across. Use the stiff, slightly moist #10 to blend this white line into the pastel green one which forms its upper border.

Feathering the tummy area comes next. Using a #1 brush, paint fat, red oxide feather shapes on the top two bands of color. Place three or four of these red oxide ovals in the top band of color and four or five in the yellow oxide band. Stagger the feathers as shown in the accompanying diagram. Now, use white paint and the #1 brush to paint three or four

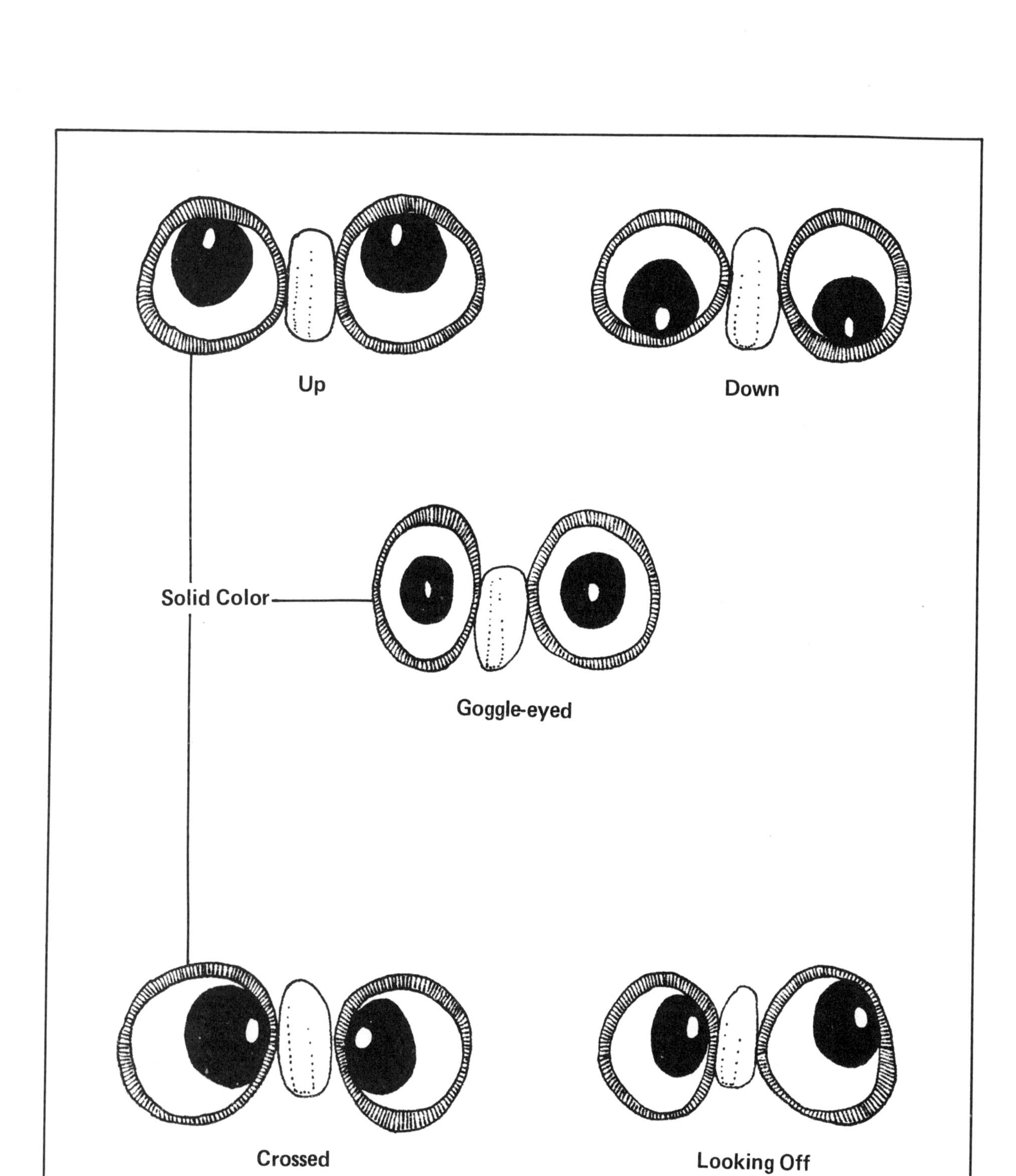

OWL EYES

white feathers in the pastel green area, again staggering the feathers as shown in the drawing.

Using black acrylic and a #000 brush, make a single arrow, pointing downward, in each oval. Then add two or three markings to represent feather veins. Make the markings lighter in the top portion of each shaft.

When feathering has been completed, paint the owl's claws by using the #000 brush to outline three red oxide triangles, pointing downward, on the top of each foot rock. Fill in these triangles and allow them to dry. Then use the #000 and black acrylic to make two small, up-curving lines in each triangle.

Now begin work on the owl's facial features by using the #000 brush to paint his beak with red oxide. Work carefully, being sure to cover the beak well, and adding a second coat if necessary.

Using the #1 brush, apply white paint to the eyes; working to the outer edges yet leaving a slight rim of darker tone. If you keep white paint on the flat surface of the eye and avoid moving over the rounded edge, you will achieve the desired effect. Try to match up the two eyes as closely as possible. Two or more coats will be needed to ensure adequate coverage.

When the final coat of white has dried, use the #000 brush to outline a black pupil onto the white area of each eye. The pupils may be slightly crossed or set so the owl will be looking up, down, or to one side or the other as shown in the accompanying drawings. They may even be made to stare straight ahead in a goggle-eyed effect. When the outlines seem symmetrical, fill them in completely with black.

As the drawing indicate your choice of eye direction will determine which edge of the pupil will be bordered in avocado green. (yellow oxide + chromium green). When the black pupils have dried, apply a border of avocado green at the appropriate edge of each. Then use the #000 brush to superimpose a white dot on each pupil, giving the eyes a lively sparkle.

Now, check the entire owl for any blemishes that need retouching and do necessary touch-ups before spraying the owl with plastic fixative according to the directions under "Spraying the Figures" in Part I.

Since owls are usually relatively heavy and since the foot rocks may be rough enough to scratch furniture or floors, cut out bits of felt in the same shape as and just smaller than the bottom surface of each foot. Lay the owl on his back, use your index finger to apply several light dabs of glue to each felt piece and press the felt firmly into place, smoothing it as you press. Set the owl on his newly felted feet and allow him to dry in this position.

This black and red graduation owl, with his boldly printed date and saucy mortarboard, is a permanent reminder of a very special occasion.

The Graduation Owl. Painting the graduation owl is considerably easier than painting the plain owl, since no feathering of the tummy portion is required. You only have to choose the predominant school color for the basic shade, add accents in a secondary color, print school initials and graduation year on the owl's chest, and glue on a mortarboard of black or white felt.

You'll need #10, #1, and #000 brushes, black and white acrylics, plus acrylics to make the two or three school colors. You'll also need to buy the small white or black felt mortarboard, the kind used for graduation party favors. Making the cap from rock might be feasible, but only if you happened to find a thin square of slate or some comparable rock.

Usually the darker, more subdued school color should be used for all areas except feet, beak, and tummy. If the predominant color has been used to tint the modeling paste, the owl's feathered areas should be relatively easy to cover.

The head, wings, and body of a graduation owl are first painted with the predominant color. These areas are actually painted, not streaked or washed, as in the case of the antiqued owl. Be sure to get the paint into all chipped or pitted areas, and use two coats if necessary.

Next, paint the feet, tummy, and beak in the second school color. Use the #1 or #000 brush in close areas around feet, neck, shoulders, and eyes, but smooth out the tops of feet and the broad areas of the tummy with the #10 brush. Note that the tummy area is a rounded section similar to that of the bear.

Next, use the #10 brush and a minimum of paint to highlight the owl's feathered areas with the second school color. Brush wings, back, and head lightly with this color, being careful to *tip*, not paint these areas. Tip only the modeling paste areas, not the smooth portion of the rocks. If you smear excess color in some spots or onto the smooth areas which contain no modeling paste, retouch these areas with the first color.

Now, move to the facial features, using the #1 brush to apply white paint to the eyes. Work right to the outer edges, yet leave a slight rim of the predominant color. If you keep the white paint on the flat surface of the eye and avoid moving over the rounded edge, you'll achieve the desired effect. Try to match up the two eyes as closely as possible. Two or more coats will be needed to ensure adequate coverage.

When the final coat of white has dried, use the #000 brush and black acrylic to outline the two pupils. Refer to the drawings of different eyes in the preceding section. When the outlines seem symmetrical, fill them in completely with black.

While the pupils are drying, use the #000 brush to give the personal touch by writing the high school or college initials across the top portion of the owl's chest and the graduation year underneath.

Use this same #000 brush to fashion black claws by outlining three triangles with curved sides, on the top of each foot rock so that they appear to be pointing downward. Fill in these triangles, allow them to dry, and then use the #000 brush and red to make two small, up-curving lines in each claw.

Move from toes to top and use the #000 brush to put a sparkle in the owl's eyes by adding a white dot to each. Make a final check for scratches or blemishes, do necessary retouching, and spray on the plastic fixative, following instructions and precautions given under "Spraying The Figures." Then felt the feet, as instructed toward the end of the section on the antiqued owl.

Once the owl's protective coat has dried, you can apply the felt mortarboard. Try several positions before deciding which one looks best. Don't worry when you discover the cap doesn't really fit. You'll be able to mold it into place with glue.

Lightly coat the inner edges of the cap portion of the mortarboard with glue and set the cap on the head. Place the index and second finger of each hand under the mortarboard and on each side of the glue-lined cap portion and apply pressure to this part of the cap. Using firm pressure and a slightly rolling motion of the fingers, mold the cap to the head.

Now allow adequate drying time (about one day) and you'll find the cap will be a permanent part of a graduation owl of lasting significance to that very special senior.

The Natural Owl. Since the natural Daystone owls have been made of round granite rocks, they display a beautiful black and white mottling on their unpainted portions. For this reason, black and white are the only acrylics used in designing this owl. If your natural rocks have other hues, choose acrylic shades that complement them, modifying the basic technique given below to fit your special needs.

Black and white acrylics and #000, #1, and #10 red sable brushes are needed for a granite owl. Choose other acrylics for owls with other natural hues.

Using black, or a color that matches the darkest natural shading in body and head rocks, and a #10 brush, cover the modeling-paste areas of head, wings, and body. This same color, of course, should have been used earlier to tint the modeling paste with which you feathered the owl. Paint carefully, avoiding smearing onto the smooth surfaces you intend to leave in their natural state.

Following the same light, brushing technique described for tipping feathered areas with red and yellow oxide on the antiqued owl, tip the natural owl's feathered areas in gray. Do not apply gray to the smooth parts of the body.

Next, use a #000 brush to paint beak and feet black, again being careful to avoid getting acrylic onto the natural surface of head and body rocks. This is especially tedious in the eye and beak areas.

When the feet have dried, use the #000 brush and white paint to form claws by outlining three triangles, tips downward, on the top of each foot rock. Fill in these triangles with white, allow them to dry, and then use a #000 brush and black paint to make two small, upcurving lines on each claw.

Feathering the tummy area comes next. Use no preliminary shading; simply make faint white feather shapes over the tummy area, making about three rows of four feathers each and staggering the feathers in the rows, as in the drawing in the section on the antiqued owl. In this case, the feather shapes should be deliberately blurred and indistinct.

Now use a #000 brush and black acrylic to sketch very light markings onto each feather oval. Make these blurred and indistinct, also, giving the desired effect without detracting from the rock's natural finish.

Move to the eyes next, using a #1 brush to apply white paint to each eye rock. Work right to the outer edges of the front of the rock, but leaving a stripe of the dark, natural surface around the edge. If you keep the white paint on the flat surface of the eye and avoid moving over the rounded edge, you'll achieve the desired effect. Try to match up the two eyes as closely as possible. Two or more coats will be needed to ensure adequate coverage.

When the final coat of white has dried, use the #000 brush and black acrylic to outline the two pupils. They may be slightly crossed or set so the owl is looking off to one side or the other. Refer to the drawings of the eyes in the section on the antiqued owl. When the outlines seem symmetrical, fill in the pupils completely with black.

When the black pupils have completely dried, use the #000 to superimpose a white dot in each eye, giving them a lively sparkle. Make a final check for scratches or blemishes, do necessary retouching, and prepare to spray your owl, observing all precautions given in the "Spraying The Figures" section.

In addition, remember that unpainted rocks tend to absorb fixative in much the same manner that unfinished wood absorbs stain. Excessive coating with spray can lead to a coated, glossed-over look which destroys the natural effect you've worked to preserve. Once over lightly should bring out the grain of the rocks and cause the colors to deepen and take on added richness, thus displaying nature's own handiwork to best advantage.

To avoid scratching tabletops or floors, felt the natural owl's feet, using the simple process outlined in the section on the antiqued owl.

Whether you've antiqued an owl, painted one in school colors, or left uncovered the natural beauty of granite or some other stones, your rockcrafted owl should be an artistic achievement in which you can take pride.

Duck

Stately mallards or downy-looking white or yellow ducklings are among the most appealing rockcraft items described in this book. Create a large mallard to grace a hearth or design a pair of ducklings to add a bright spot to bathroom, kitchen, or nursery.

Choosing The Rocks

Obviously, the size of your creation must be considered when you choose rocks for any figure. Deciding on size before you start rock hunting can save time. What options do you have for the size of a duck?

Very large rocks can become another Herniatia, Jere Day's 100-pound lawn duck, so named for obvious reasons! One step down in size leads to the construction of a 12- to 15-inch mallard for hearth or garden or a yellow duckling doorstop for the nursery.

Still smaller (6 or 8 inches) mallards are popular mantel and coffee-table items, though white and yellow ducklings of this size don't seem to appeal as well as those of larger or smaller dimensions. Smaller ducklings are most attractive when two of slightly different size are paired on a single base rock. Miniature mallards on pieces of rough rock or driftwood make attractive terrarium figures.

Once you've made up your mind as to the size duck you wish to make, decide whether your finished duck will be mallard or duckling in order to choose rocks best suited for one design or the other. Before choosing which you'll make, consider that mallard ducks, though fairly easy to glue and shape with modeling paste, present an artistic challenge of a different sort than that presented by the simpler objects described in this book. Here a rockcrafter tries to capture natural coloration in a way not demanded of his caricatured turtles or ladybugs. For those who prefer to hold to the simpler lines of caricature, yellow and white ducklings offer the advantage of working well in groupings, designed to fit their personality.

The body rock of a mallard may be an oval similar to the body of a reclining bear, but with one end (the tail portion) more tapered than the other. A shorter oval (almost ladybug shape) is better for a duckling, since the fat, downy body of a duckling is more readily seen in a rock of this shape.

For mallards, a smooth, elongated rock with one end slightly tapered makes a realistic head rock. The tapered end makes an excellent bill. Duckling heads may be similar to those of a mallard, but the duckling's face can have a broader surface. Perfect head rocks should probably be saved for the more realistic mallards.

The broad, webbed feet of a duck can be made from flat, smooth rocks which are relatively elliptical in shape. Again, reserve the most realistic foot rocks for mallards; fat feet which might add personality to a downy duckling would detract from the overall appearance of a mallard.

Herniatia gives a ride to a friend as a saucy caterpillar looks on.

For ducks of 10 inches or longer, modeling-paste tails will be easier to build up if a rock tail is glued on first. The broken ends of mushroom stem rocks (described later in the book) make excellent tail rocks, but any stubby, fat rock with one relatively flat surface will do.

Set the rocks together, trying for a satisfactory fit before deciding which rocks will make up a particular duck. Keep looking until you find rocks that will make gluing and painting easier for you.

The Gluing

Once appropriate rocks have been chosen for mallards or ducklings, gluing of both variations is very similar.

Materials. The rough working surface, glue, glue sticks, and props described in the turtle section are also used for assembling ducks. In addition, you will need two cylindrical rocks of similar size and weight to prop the sides of the duck's head during the drying period. For molding the duck's tail you'll need unshaded modeling paste, a palette knife, and a damp cloth or paper towel.

Procedure—Rocks. Place the two foot rocks side by side but angled outward, to give a waddling effect. Slightly exaggerating this outward thrust adds a comic effect to a duckling, but detracts from the mallard's stateliness.

If you're working on a mallard, remember that the body rock's more tapered end will become its tail. Put the body rock onto foot rocks and balance it there. Then try placing the head, remembering to put the tapered end outward and to let the long sides of the rock form the sides of the head. Now try to determine whether or not the weight of the head rests so that the duck's center of gravity is correct for upright posture. If the head's weight shifts that center too far forward, the duck will fall on his bill when the glue has dried and the props are removed.

If the duck does seem head-heavy, try a different position for the body by pushing the body rock farther back on the feet. Now, try the head again to see whether your duck is still tipsy.

A mallard such as this one makes a fine hearth ornament for fireplace or Franklin stove.

Place a generous dab of glue on each foot; then press the body rock gently but firmly into place in the balanced position. Get props ready, including the oblong propping rocks you've chosen. Test the head position once more to be sure the finished duck won't be head-heavy and to see exactly where head and body will be joined.

Place a generous dab of glue on the head rock, and press the head into place. Use your index finger to wipe excess glue from the neck area, since you'll need a smooth surface on which to paint the mallard's white neck ring. Trimming dried glue later with a razor blade won't make a smooth enough surface for a neat neck ring.

Large ducks should have additional glue applied to the neck area after the first glue has dried long enough to turn almost clear. Use your index finger to apply a film of glue all around the area where head and body rock meet, ensuring a good seal. When this film dries clear, apply glue again, continuing to build up the neck area so that head and body will remain together long after the last coat of paint has been applied.

Place a stack of wood scraps and/or poker chips under the duck's head so that the head rock stays at the correct height. Place a heavy propping rock on each side of the head rock to keep the duck looking in the right direction. Preventing sagging or tilting is essential if the finished duck is to be well enough balanced to stand on its own.

A tail rock may be needed for large ducks, since forming modeling paste tails of considerable size is easier if paste is applied over an area already heightened by a rock. Building large tails from modeling paste alone is an extremely tedious and time-consuming process, since the paste must be built up, layer after layer, with adequate drying time allowed for between layers. Without this layering, the tails will sag and slip. Even when such care is taken, the layers tend to form unsightly cracks as they dry. Any round or oval rock will do, but one with one slightly concave side is ideal, since the concave surface fits close to the body rock and allows for easy gluing. The rounded, broken ends of mushroom stems, as

White or yellow love ducks are popular rock items.

Chips, wood scraps, and a pair of heavy cylindrical rocks are all needed to hold the duck's head in place during the drying process.

described in a later section, make perfect tail rocks.

Place a liberal dab of thick glue on the tail rock and press the rock into place on top of and near the end of the body rock. No props should be needed, and excess glue will be covered with modeling paste.

Procedure—Modeling-Paste Tail. Since paste must be of the proper consistency if you are to make satisfactory duck tails, you may wish to try the half-and-half mixture suggested under "Modeling Paste" in Part I. No acrylic paint is added to this paste, since the areas of the tail most prone to chipping (edges and tip) will be painted white.

Small mallards and small ducklings may have tails made entirely of modeling paste. For either of these ducks, use a palette knife to place the appropriate amount of paste on the end of the body rock. Pull the knife away in an upward and outward motion, leaving a thick, conical tail. Use the palette knife to shape the tail feathers, applying more paste if necessary.

Larger ducks require the use of tail rocks like the one described in the preceding section. To cover a rock tail, use the palette knife to place a large blob of paste behind the tail rock. If you're making a mallard and you plan to leave his back in its natural rock finish, be sure to avoid smearing excess paste onto his back. Look at a picture of the finished mallard to see just where tail ends and back begins before you apply any modeling paste to the tail area.

Using the palette knife, sweep the paste upward from the base of the tail, achieving the basic tail shape. Keep a damp cloth handy for cleaning the knife when it becomes too filled with paste to allow easy working of the tail. When the basic shaping has been done, get rid of rough palette marks by smoothing the tail with a finger dipped in water. Then use the palette knife to make curly little feathers on the outer, upper edges of the tail. Pinch the end of the tail to a point for ducklings; for mallards, curve that point slightly forward.

If you're making a duck over 10 inches in length, you may need to apply another layer or two of modeling paste in order to build up the tail to desired size and shape. Be sure to allow ample drying time between layers (overnight, in most cases). When applying the final layer, make curly little feathers on the outer, upper edges of the tail and use a wet finger to make the tail's underside as smooth as possible.

Sometimes modeling paste tails start to sag and slide down too low in the rear. To offset this tendency, a duck may be picked up, tipped nose down, and gently shaken a few times until the tail moves into place. To be sure it doesn't slide again, let the duck stand on its nose until the paste is completely dry.

If you're creating a mallard 10 inches long or longer, you may wish to add a little authenticity, by using a real mallard tail feather for building the modeling-paste one. Hunters will probably be glad to give you the twin tail feathers from mallards bagged during the duck season.

Once you have built up the tail with modeling paste and smoothed it with a damp finger, you're ready to add a single feather. Cut the feather off so that you leave the curling tip plus just enough of the shaft to fit securely into the modeling paste tail. The length you leave the feather depends, of course, on the size of the mallard you're making.

Now, insert the feather about one inch from the tip of the modeling paste tail with feather tip curling upward and back toward the duck's head. Then, because a single, fragile feather would detract from the naturalness of a rockcrafted mallard, you will need to cover the feather with modeling paste. Following the general shape of the curving feather, apply modeling paste until the feather is covered. Use enough paste to coat the feather, but not enough to make it so heavy its tip droops down and touches the duck's body.

Once this feather has been coated with paste and arranged to your satisfaction, allow the duck to dry overnight before adding a final layer of paste to the main portion of the tail. Use the palette knife to form the curly outer tail feathers, and a damp finger to smooth out the tail's underside.

Paint the Duck

Having chosen either mallard or duckling, proceed according to the painting instructions in one of the two sections below. Before beginning to paint either variation, check for cracks which may have formed in the modeling-paste tail. Use a palette knife to apply modeling paste to cracked area. Use your index finger to push the paste into the cracks.

Tail rocks should be used with all ducks of 10 inches or longer and may also be used with smaller ducks.

Chart I:

Color mixing chart for the mallard

BASIC COLORS	SHADE
White + small amount of black	= light gray
Cadmium orange + yellow oxide	= yellow orange
White + black + small amount of burnt umber	= dark gray
Burnt sienna	= burnt sienna
Phthalocyanine green + permanent green light	= bright mallard green
Burnt umber	= burnt umber
White + black + fairly large amount of burnt umber	= brownish gray
Phthalocyanine blue + white	= deep blue
White + yellow oxide	= beige
Yellow oxide + permanent green light	= greenish yellow
Chromium oxide green + yellow oxide + white	= light avocado

The Mallard. When trial-and-error efforts based on looking at photos and paintings of ducks failed to yield the desired patterning, Jere Day turned to a friend's family heirloom—a forty-year-old, hand-carved, hand-painted mallard decoy. Once successful in luring ducks to within a few yards of hunters' blinds, the old decoy's final service was to provide the perfect pattern for Jere's rockcrafted mallards. The result? Rockcrafted mallards in great demand with hunters and birdwatchers—people whose years of close observation of waterfowl in the wild make them an excellent judge of authenticity of reproduction.

Achieving this authenticity requires the mixing of several colors. For best results, all these colors should be mixed before painting begins and stored in tightly covered containers as described under "Paints and Brushes" in Part I. For convenience later on, label the color it contains. Since retouching is a must, you should be sure to mix enough paint to be sure the exact shade will be ready when retouching is done. To make maximum use of the mixed acrylics, make several mallards at one time.

Follow Chart I when mixing mallard hues. Chart II shows where on the duck each shade is used.

Once you have mixed the colors given in Chart I, you can use Chart II to tell at a glance the colors needed for each part of the mallard. As you read the following paragraphs, refer frequently to the photos of the finished mallards and to Chart II.

A light gray base coat is applied first—unless the body rock has color and texture

Chart II:

Uses for the mallard's colors (approximately in order used)

USE	SHADE
Base coat for body rock	light gray
Feet	yellow orange
Back	dark gray (may be solid, natural, or sponge mottled)
Dark line in center back	black
Breast	burnt sienna
Head	bright mallard green
Wings	
forewing	burnt umber
wing tip	brownish gray
mid section	deep blue
reclining teardrop	beige mottled with burnt umber
Bill	greenish yellow
Pupil outline	light avocado

that warrant using the natural surface instead of an acrylic finish. If you've chosen the natural back, use the #1 brush and light gray paint to draw a line that starts at the tip of the tail and follows the feathered edges of the tail forward. Extend the line along the duck's body in approximately the place where the water line would come if your mallard were taking a swim. End the line toward the duck's breast bone. (Don't be confused by the photos of the finished mallards, which show a half-circle of color extending below the swim line on the duck's breast. Go ahead and draw a complete swim line; the breast will be painted over it later.) Now, paint the body rock light gray *below* this swim line (including tummy or underside) and leave the area above the swim line in its natural state.

If you've chosen to paint the entire body rock, no line need be drawn at this time, though this same line will later be used to determine where to place the bottom of the duck's wing and to determine how far down to apply the dark gray of the back. Paint the entire body rock light gray at this time, excluding the head and feet.

The feet are now painted a bright yellow orange. Use a #1 brush, unless closeness of feet to body rock makes a #000 brush necessary. Start with tops and edges of the feet, making sure to cover all glued areas. Then move to the bottoms and allow the mallard to dry on his head. After a few minutes' drying time, apply a second coat, if necessary, remembering that poorly covered rocks make poorly crafted ducks. For large ducks use a #10 brush, after edging with a #1 brush, since the #10 yields a smoother surface.

The back, the next section to be painted, may be done in three different ways. To create the natural look, do not apply any paint at this time. For a solid, dark gray back, use a #1 brush to draw on the swim line described above. Then paint all the body rock above that line dark gray. Apply a second coat with a #10 brush to make a smoother back.

For the mottled look, dip a small sponge in dark gray, dab the sponge on a newspaper

By curving down from bisecting line back toward the tail, then down and forward to meet the swim line, the brush has outlined the upper portion of the mallard's tail area. The line being drawn to the right will complete the outline.

or paper plate until just enough paint remains to leave a mottled or speckled impression. Then dab the sponge lightly onto the light gray base, mottling only the upper half of the mallard's body rock. To be sure you don't go below the swim line, you might wish to draw in this line, using a #000 brush and dark gray. The line you draw for a guide now will later be covered by the wing lines.

Other than the basic color of the back, the other features of natural, solid, and mottled ducks are all painted in the same way. Using a #000 brush and, as Chart II indicates, black paint, start at the back of the neck and draw a line that bisects the duck's back and ends at the tip of his tail. This line must be almost perfectly centered on his back. If you're using a natural-finish back, be especially careful to get the line right the first time, since no coverup is possible without hiding the rock's surface.

Next, starting at a point on the bisecting line and two-thirds of the way back from the neck to the tip of the tail, curve down and back to a point about five-sixths of the way back from the neck. At this point, curve the tapered line down and forward to meet the swim line. Then, changing direction, extend the line back, along the swim line, to under the tail. Repeat for the other side, letting the two lines meet under the tail.

Once the outline has been painted on, the bisecting line should be widened a bit using black paint and a #000 brush, from the neck back to the point where it branches and starts to curve down. The tail area outlined by the branching lines should then be painted black, as should the tail's outlined underside. White edging will be added at a later time.

The breast is painted next, using a #1 brush and burnt sienna. Starting at the center back point of the neck, draw a line which tapers down and around to the center front. Repeat for the other side, making the two lines meet to form a shape similar to a round baby's bib. Keep working until the right and left sides are symmetrical; then with burnt sienna fill in the breast line starting at the lower line and moving up to the neck line.

A mallard's bright green head is a ready

This close-up of a finished mallard shows the four parts of the wing. The top wing segment is a beige reclining tear drop. Other segments, from left to right, are the forewing, midsection, and wing tip.

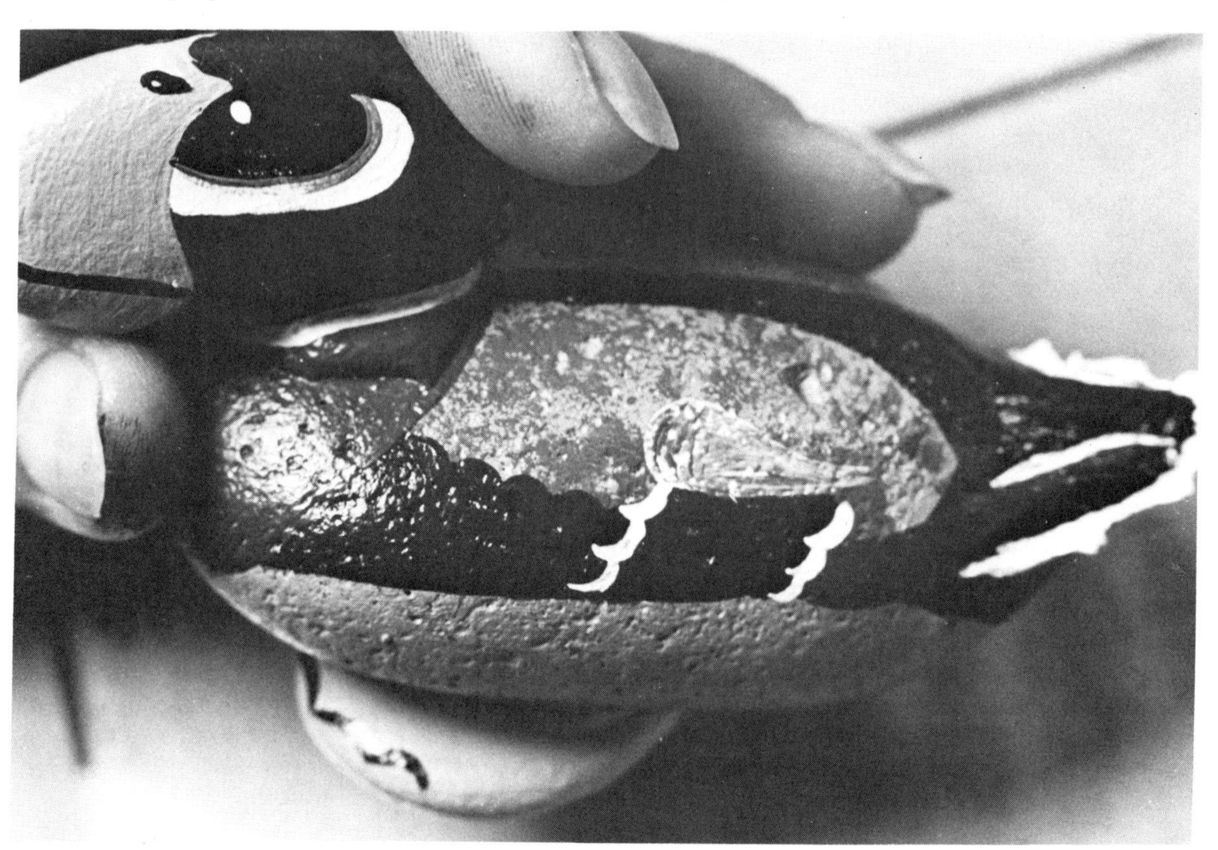

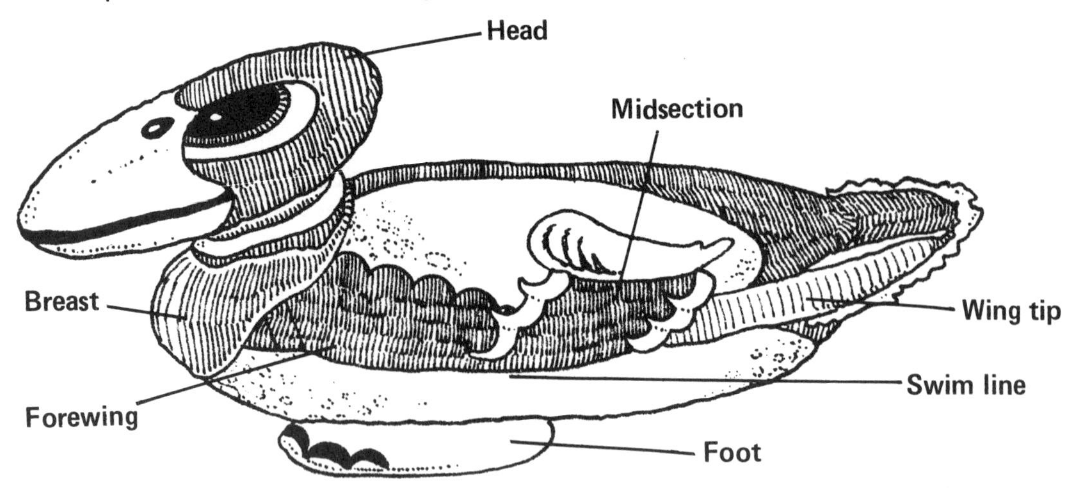

mark of identification for birdwatchers and hunters. Using a #1 brush and starting above the burnt sienna line at the center back of the neck, paint the entire head rock mallard green. Be especially careful to paint right to the sienna line *under* the head, too. A nearly perfect line is needed where breast and neck meet, since a white collar ring will be added at this juncture.

Once the close work of the first coat has been done, smooth over the head with a #10 brush. Allow a few moments' drying time and apply a second coat, again using #1 or #000 brush in close areas and #10 for smoothing the broader areas of the head.

The four different wing sections are now painted in this order: forewing, wing tip, wing midsection, and reclining-teardrop section. Before beginning work on these individual sections, study the close up of the completed wing so that you can see how all sections fit together.

The forewing is outlined in burnt umber, using a #000 brush and beginning at a point where the swim line meets the curve of the breast. Following the curve of the breast, paint a thin line from swim line to a point about one-third the way from swim line to the center back of the neck.

Then, starting again where swim line meets the breast line, paint a line that follows the swim line to about one-third the distance between the burnt sienna breast and the tip of the mallard's tail, as shown in the drawing.

If you have previously outlined the swim line in gray, be sure this new line of burnt umber covers the old gray line. Now, starting with the highest one nearest the breast, paint on scallops to simulate feathers, and fill in underneath, down to the swim line, to complete the forewing.

The wing-tip section is painted next, using a #000 brush and brownish gray. Starting near the tip of the tail, outline a longhorn shape which meets the swim line on the bottom and is slightly narrower than the forewing. Extend this rear wing tip nearly to the forewing, since you want to avoid leaving a blank space where this tip meets the midsection.

The wing midsection should be outlined in deep blue. Use the #000 brush to make a

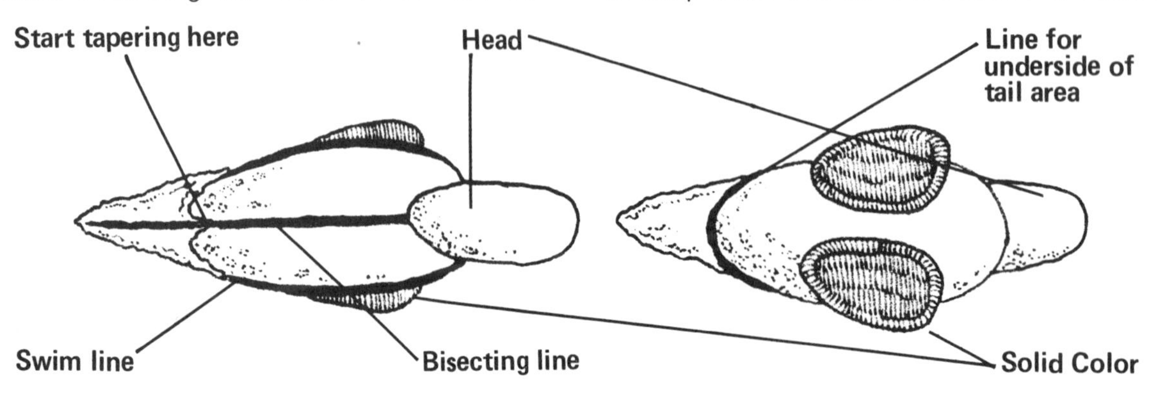

three-part wavy line, like three parentheses stacked up, at the rear edge of the burnt umber forewing and perpendicular to the swim line. Then make another at the front edge of the rear wing tip. These lines should extend a fraction above both forewing and rear wing tip but not below the swim line. Join the wavy lines with a bottom line and a top line, making sure the bottom line covers any gray paint that may have been used to outline the swim line earlier. Fill in the outlined midsection with deep blue.

Next, use the #000 brush to outline the outside edges of the wavy lines of the midsection in black. After sufficient drying time, outline the outside black edges of both three-part wavy lines in white. With the #000 brush, edge the top of the brownish-gray wing tip in white, starting at the tip and extending the white line forward, nearly to the halfway point on the brownish-gray portion of the wing.

Further white-trim work is now in order. Using the #000 brush and starting at the very tip of the tail, dab the outer edges of the top of the tail in white. Taper off the paint line to end a bit before you reach the swim line. Uneven dabs help to give a ruffled-feather look. When the top has been edged, turn over the mallard and tip the bottom edges in white, starting at the tip of his tail and stopping where the white edging for the top side ends.

The final section of the wing is a beige portion shaped like a reclining teardrop whose tip points slightly upward and whose wider portion is forward. This beige wing section is placed above the deep-blue midsection so that the front curve and rear tip of the teardrop extend just a fraction beyond the front and rear portions of the midsection of the wing.

Using a #000 brush and beige paint, and beginning with the rear tip, outline the reclining teardrop. Then fill in with beige. Before the beige has dried, dip the #000 brush in burnt umber and wipe the paint onto a newspaper or a paper plate until a minimum of paint remains on the brush. Blend this darker paint with the beige, giving the teardrop a mottled appearance.

Painting the mallard's facial features, should begin with the bill. Starting about halfway down the middle of the head rock, make a deep scallop across the top portion of the head and centered, using a #000 brush and greenish-yellow paint. Bring down half scallops on either side of this scallop and continue them in the same curve down to a point two-thirds of the way down the side of the head rock, as shown in the accompanying drawing. Proceed by starting a new scallop that makes a line under the bill to the centerpoint underneath. Outline the other side of the bill in the same manner, so that the two lines meet under the head rock. Work for symmetry; then fill in the outlined area in greenish yellow. Two coats will probably be necessary to ensure good coverage.

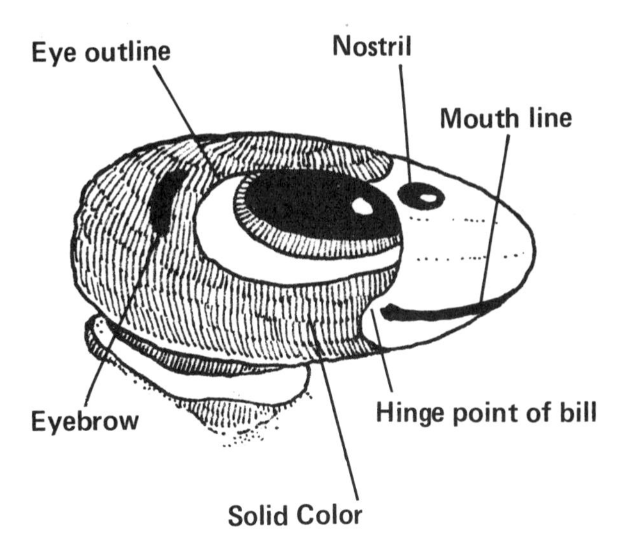

While the bill is drying, paint two black eyebrows, using a #000 brush. Note that the position of these eyebrows is more vertical than horizontal, and be sure to get them even.

Although the rockcrafted mallard is intended to be a fairly realistic representation of a duck, the eyes are deliberately caricatured. Tiny, realistic eyes seem too beady and unattractive to appeal to most buyers, and even hunters and birders consistently prefer the larger caricatured eyes.

Using the #000 brush, the mallard's eye is outlined in black by starting at the bill, moving back toward the tail, and then around to the bill again in an oval shape. The curve of the bill forms the lower part of the eye oval. An inverted-teardrop–shaped nostril is outlined in black just beneath each point of the bill.

Use the #000 brush and black acrylic to start the mouth line at the center front portion of the bill and work around one side to the apex of the scallops on that side of the bill. Repeat for the other side of the mouth.

Use a #000 or #1 brush to fill in the white of the eyeball, applying two or more coats to ensure adequate coverage and smoothing with a #10 if necessary. When the final coat of white has dried, use the #000 brush to outline black oval pupils, making the duck seem to be looking up at you. Work to make both pupils the same size and shape, then fill in the outlined areas with black.

When the black paint has dried, edge the lower and outer portions of the pupils in avocado, starting at the point where pupil meets bill and moving around the pupil's outer edge to the point where pupil meets the bright green of the head.

Use the #000 brush to place a dot of white in each eye and to draw the white neck ring. Start the ring at centerback of neck and move around one side to the midway point under the head rock. Repeat for the other side. Then broaden the line to the desired width and add as many coats as necessary to achieve a distinct neck ring. Allow the white to dry thoroughly, and then retouch the burnt sienna and green along the neck ring.

The duck's webbed toes are the final painting step. Four simple inverted scallops as seen in photos of the finished mallards are outlined in black on each foot, using a #000 brush.

Now that you've finished creating a realistic mallard from mere rocks, don't spoil the overall effect by neglecting to do necessary touching up. Since the swim line is, by now, quite uneven, retouch this line with the light gray used for the base coat. When retouching has been done, sign your name or initials on the duck's underside and apply a satin-sheen finish according to the instructions for spraying the fixative in Part I.

The Duckling. Easier to paint than the simplest turtle, the downy duckling requires few instructions for an experienced rockcrafter.

Start by using a #10 brush to apply a gesso base coat over body and head rocks. When the gesso has dried, apply two coats of yellow oxide acrylic for a yellow duckling or two coats of white for a white duckling. Use the stiff bristles of a #10 brush to edge the tip of a white duck's tail in orange (cadmium orange). Edge the tip of a yellow duck's tail in cadmium red light. Paint the duckling's feet to match his tail trim.

Facial features of the downy duckling are similar to those of the mallard, but his bill has only one peak between the eyes. Using a #000 brush and the same color you used for his feet, start the single bill peak about halfway up the head rock.

Outline the edge of one side of the bill by curving down forward, then back again to the hinge point, a point halfway down the side of the head rock. Continue the bill's outline by again extending this line forward and under the bill to the centerpoint beneath the bill.

Outline the other side of the bill so that the two lines meet under the head rock. Work for symmetry, then fill in the outlined area in the same color you used for the duckling's feet. Two coats will probably be necessary to ensure good coverage.

The mouth is outlined like that of the mallard, unless you prefer to make an open mouth. Adding smile lines at the corners of a closed mouth can give a duckling a winsome personality.

The eyes are outlined like those of a mallard. If you goof a little and the eye outlines aren't drawn exactly alike, you can always draw new lines and then cover your goofs with the white of the eyeball. Use two coats of white to fill in the eyeballs, add pupils of black, and edge the pupils in blue (pthalocyanine + white). Add a sparkle by superimposing a tiny dot of white on each pupil.

Single ducklings with slightly crossed eyes can have a one-rock ladybug perched on their broad bills (see the instructions for the simple ladybug in the frog section of the book). Duckling pairs may be glued to a base rock, and modeling-paste grass with flowers added to the arrangement.

If two ducklings of the same size are given simple male and female characteristics (straight vs. curly lashes), then paired on a base rock complete with dainty flowers peeking from modeling-paste grass, you've created loveducks. Accentuate their romantic attitude by tilting them inward so that they seem to be gazing into one another's eyes and nuzzling bills.

If paired ducklings are slightly different in size, a mama-and-baby effect will likely result. Emphasize this theme by having mama give baby a lesson in worm gobbling. How? Simply tilt baby's head downward and give him an open mouth—in front of which you place a two-rock caterpillar. (See the photo of this pair earlier in this section.)

When you have glued your arrangement of ducklings, you will probably want to cover the bottom of the rough base rock with felt to prevent scratching of table tops or floors. Refer to the felting instructions given in the owl section.

After checking the finished ducklings for stray specks of paint or other blemishes, do necessary retouching, sign your name or initials in one corner of the base rock, and spray on the protective satin-sheen finish, following the directions under "Spraying The Figures" in Part I.

Your duckling grouping is now ready to brighten up bathroom, kitchen, or nursery or to adorn a flower arrangement for a friend.

Mushrooms

Mushroom groupings require the use of most of the skills learned through making the items previously described. In addition, mushrooms are usually grouped in arrangements of two or three to a base rock and often enhanced by the addition of a miniature version of one of the insects, turtles, or frogs described in the preceding pages.

bzxhethehoosino to show off a rock's natural beauty by using no base coat for your mushrooms, to paint mushrooms in earthy or pastel colors, or to antique mushroom groupings, an experienced rockcrafter will find mushroom creation a challenging and rewarding pastime.

Choosing The Rocks

A typical mushroom grouping requires five rocks, plus the ones for any insects or animals you plan to add to the arrangement. Necessary rocks include two cylindrical stem rocks, two turtle-body-type rocks for caps, and a flat, broad base rock of no particular shape.

Stem and cap rocks should be chosen with the idea of making two mushrooms of different size. The base rock should be large enough to hold both mushrooms plus grass, flowers, and perhaps a miniature insect or animal. Natural color of rocks for a grouping is usually unimportant, though paired rocks of particularly interesting color or texture can be used without base coats of acrylic paint and placed on a base rock left in its natural state.

Stem rocks should be as nearly cylindrical as possible, and fairly flat on each end to ensure successful gluing. Since cylindrical rocks with flat ends are relatively rare, the rockcrafter must usually break off the ends of cylindrical rocks to get good stem rocks.

Breaking rocks requires safety goggles, a hammer, cold chisel, and a stone, or concrete working surface. Though a smooth, fairly level break is preferable (one perpendicular to the longitudinal axis of the rock), slanted breaks occur most often. Unless the break is severely slanted, such rocks make mushroom stems that lean outward at interesting, natural-looking angles.

To break a stem rock, put on the saftey goggles, place the rock on a hard working surface, put the chisel's sharp edge on the rock along the desired break line, and strike the chisel's blunt end sharply with the hammer. Apply successively harder blows until fracture occurs. Still no break? Give up and try another rock—unless this one's become such a challenge you're willing to enlist stronger help plus a sledge hammer!

Some rocks do break more easily than others. Those with red or white shading seem to break with less pounding and more evenly. Black or very dark gray rocks tend to shatter rather than break evenly.

Break both ends of the stem rock and save the broken ends for use as owls' ears, mallards' tails, or, if small enough, bears' ears. Try setting each cap rock onto its stem to make sure cap and stem are in proper proportion.

The Gluing

Materials. The rough working surface, glue, glue sticks, and props described in the turtle section are also used for assembling mushroom groupings. In addition, you will need appropriately shaded modeling paste for the grass at the base of the mushrooms and a damp cloth on which to wipe fingers after gluing and after using the modeling paste.

Procedure—Rocks. Successful gluing of mushroom groupings requires the use of unusually thick glue. Refer to the paragraphs on gluing in the turtle section for an easy method of bringing thinner glue to the desired consistency. Thick glue applied in necessarily generous amounts may take up to one week to dry thoroughly. This drying time is particularly disconcerting because mushrooms must be glued and dried in several stages. Don't try to proceed with other steps until the white glue has turned almost completely clear; sagging mushrooms usually part company with their bases and/or readily lose their caps. Gluing several groupings together can make being patient during the drying time somewhat easier.

Step one is to glue the stems to the caps. Get large wood scraps ready to use as props. Then place a mushroom cap on the gluing board, leaving the flatter side up. Apply a generous blob of thick glue to the stem rock, press the stem gently but firmly into place in the cap's center, and wipe off excess glue with your index finger.

Leave the mushroom upside down and prop securely in place with wooden blocks or wood scraps. Proceed with other caps and stems in the same manner, remembering to make several different sizes so that paired mushrooms will be of uneven heights.

Now, set aside the board of mushrooms and paint other figures, bake cookies, write to your mother, take a week off for work in the flower garden—anything to keep you from disturbing those mushrooms too soon! A week's drying time is not unusual in moderately humid climates, but there is no way to hurry this process.

A simple painting step precedes the next gluing operation, except in the case of the groupings to be left in their natural state or to be antiqued. Pairing mushrooms at this point can help you to decide which ones have surface colors and textures too beautiful to be given an acrylic coating.. Also, if you plan to give an antiquing to a particular grouping, be sure to skip this next beige-paint step.

This base coat, a mixture of a small amount of yellow oxide and white, is applied to stem and cap. Apply second and third coats, if necessary, to stem and to underside

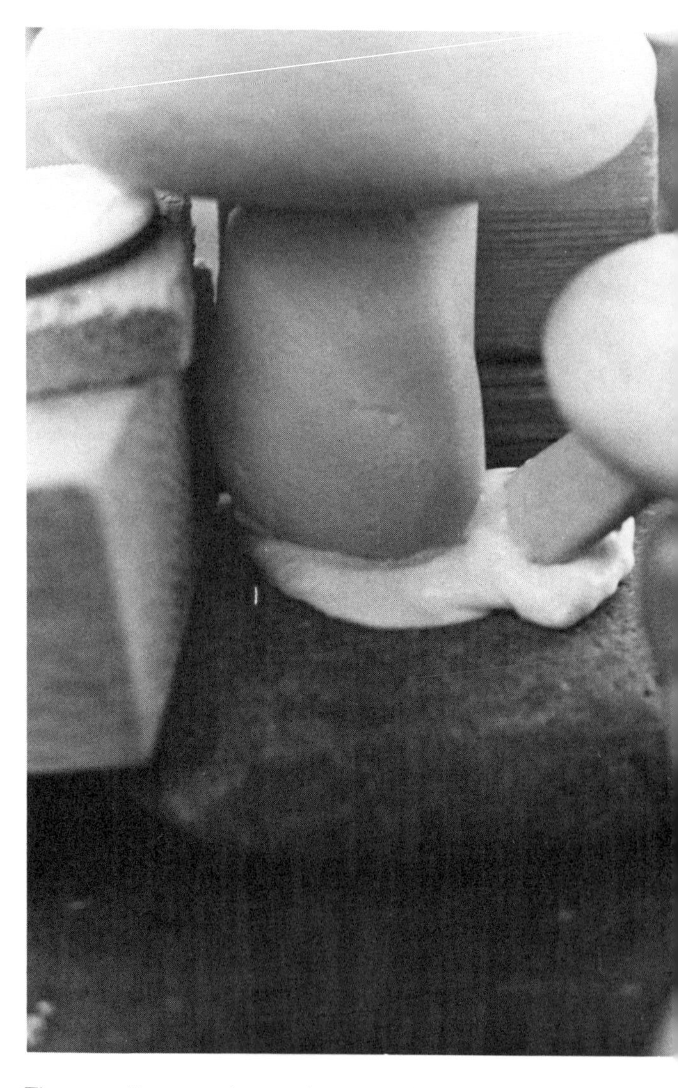

The smaller mushroom's stem barely touches that of the larger one.

of cap. Since the top of the cap is to be painted a different color, one coat of creamy beige is sufficient to ensure that the beige extends far enough up the sides of the cap to make retouching along this color seam unnecessary.

Pairs of mushrooms are now glued to the base rock you've chosen. Place the base rock, flatter side down, on the gluing board. Decide on a front and back side with the front side facing you. Now try placing the larger mushroom's stem on the base rock, just to the left or right of center and at the angle made necessary by the stem rock's chiseled surface.

If this angle seems too acute to be natural or to allow a satisfactory gluing job, try pushing one edge of the smaller mushroom's stem under the edge of the larger stem. If this arrangement doesn't work, try placing a tiny pebble under the edge of the larger stem to tilt the mushroom in the desired direction. Once the arrangement seems satisfactory, place a generous blob of glue on the larger stem. Be sure to use enough glue to prevent the formation of air pockets in the area between stem and base rock. If you're using a pebble for balance, push it into the glue blob, press the stem gently, but firmly, into place, and begin propping. Mushrooms often take as many as three separate bracing stacks, depending on the angle at which their stems meet the base rock's surface.

Don't worry about excess glue since this area of even natural-finish mushrooms will be covered with modeling-paste grass. Now apply glue to the bottom of the smaller stem and press this stem into place near the first one. If you need to alter the angle of the larger stem by slipping the smaller one under its edge, do so at this time. When the second mushroom's position seems satisfactory, use props to secure it during the drying process.

Again, wait until the glue is almost clear to begin the painting process. A week-long drying period may be necessary, but patience now will ensure a mushroom grouping that will not sag over just as the final spot is being painted on the cap. During the long drying time you may wish to glue and paint an insect, frog, or turtle to add to the grouping.

Procedure—Modeling Paste. Grass of appropriately shaded modeling paste adds a natural look to mushroom groupings and helps to cover the jointed area between stems and base. When deciding on a suitable modeling paste, remember the tip given under "Modeling Paste" in Part I and consider using a half-and-half mixture of two brands.

Since no paint will be used to cover the modeling-paste grass, acrylic must be added to the wet modeling paste now to achieve the desired shading. For natural-finish groupings, add a touch of black to achieve a gray that blends with the colors of base, stem, and cap rocks. For both painted and antiqued group-

Grass is made by laying a brush filled with tinted modeling paste alongside a mushroom stem so that the pointed portion of the paste forms a blade of grass along the stem and the remaining portion of the paste is left on the base rock.

ings, add chromium oxide green to the white paste.

Modeling-paste grass is applied with a #1 brush. You may choose to use an old one for this operation, though modeling paste will wash out of the brush quite easily. Dip the bristles into the paste until the wooden portion above the bristles is submerged an inch or so into the paste. Pull the brush out slowly, so that a pointed strand of paste clings to the brush.

Lay the brush alongside a mushroom stem so that the pointed portion of the paste forms a blade of grass along the stem and the remaining paste is left on the base rock. Continue this procedure until the lower portion of both stems is surrounded by grass blades that effectively hide all glued areas of the stems. A good example of the grass is seen in the frog-bedecked grouping pictured later in this section.

Now brush excess paste out from these blades and onto the base rock to cover any glue on the base rock and to complete the effect of grass. Leave the outer edges of the base rock's top surface uncovered; the grass should not come all the way to the edge of the base.

For natural-finish groupings, try to spread the modeling paste thin at the outer edges of the grass plot, blending the gray paste into the gray surface of the base rock rather than creating a distinct line where grass patch ends and rock surface begins.

Modeling paste applied this thick should be allowed to dry for several hours—preferably overnight—to avoid fingerprints in the wet paste or smeared paste onto other areas of stem or base rocks.

Painting the Mushrooms

Rocks that will be left in their natural state require the addition of cap spots, stem markings, and flowers in the modeling-paste grass. Other groupings call for a creamy-beige base coat for stem and underside of cap, a bright or pastel base coat for the top of the cap, plus painted cap spots, stem markings, and flowers in the modeling-paste grass. A third

Cadmium red light spots and stem markings, gray modeling-paste grass with white flowers, and a rockcrafted ladybug brighten this natural-finish mushroom grouping.

option involves antiquing the caps, stems, and base after raised cap spots have been formed with modeling paste. Choose one of these variations and follow the step-by-step instructions provided.

The Natural Look. Mushrooms to be left in their natural state should be made from rocks whose color and texture are rich and interesting. For such rocks no base coat is used, and colors for cap spots and stem markings are usually chosen that are appropriate to whatever insect will be placed on cap or base rock.

Since ladybugs are especially well suited for use with natural groupings, cadmium red light spots and stem markings can be used to good advantage. Use a #1 brush to outline five circles of red around the outer rim of the top side of the cap. Several circles of varied sizes will also be needed in the center portion of any cap on which no insect or animal is to be placed. Fill in these circles with cadmium red light.

While the red spots are drying, use cadmium red acrylic and a #000 brush to make a few "wishbone" markings along each stem. The line forming the longer side of the wishbone may be a bit thicker than the other line. Using a #000 brush and black acrylic, outline the wishbone's outer edges in black, as shown in the photograph.

Then use the #000 brush to outline one-half of each of the red cap spots. Either half may be outlined but be consistent in which side you choose to outline for all spots in a mushroom grouping. To make this black rim, start with light brush pressure at the top, apply more pressure to thicken the line near the spot's middle portion, and again lighten pressure and thin the line as you move downward.

If the base rock has black markings on its natural surface, you might tip the high spots in the modeling-paste grass with black paint on a #1 brush. Flowers for a natural grouping may be added in the gray modeling-paste grass at the base of each mushroom. Four dots of white form the petals, and a dot of red serves as the center for each flower. A random spacing of these flowers in the grass finishes the basic painting for a natural grouping.

Set a ladybug (glued and painted according to the instructions for the ladybug earlier in the book) on top of one cap or on the base rock. When you've decided on a suitable resting spot for this bug, apply glue to her four feet and press her gently, but firmly, into place.

Allow her to dry until the glue is nearly clear before checking the finished grouping for stray specks of paint or other blemishes. Do necessary retouching (though this is limited on a natural grouping), sign your name or initial in one corner of the base rock, and then follow the instructions under "Spraying The Figures" to give the grouping a protective satin sheen. Be aware that the spray will change the rocks' color, since bare rock surface rapidly absorbs the spray. An even, single application of spray will usually bring out the rock's surface characteristics in much the same way that applying stain to wood brings out the natural grain. Also, just as staining darkens wood, spraying natural-finish rocks darkens them. Spraying too heavily can cause the rocks to darken too much or to lose their naturalness by becoming too shiny.

Mushroom arrangements are almost always rough enough to warrant use of felt padding to protect furniture. Use green felt and follow the directions for felting in the owl section.

The Bright or Pastel Look. Rocks whose natural color and texture are not outstanding enough to warrant leaving them bare, or rocks with pitted places which must be patched and smoothed with modeling paste should receive the creamy-beige base coat described under "Procedure—Rocks" in this section.

Try painting mushrooms to fit kitchen or bathroom decor. Paint bright or pastel caps and apply cap spots and stem markings of complementary shades. While larger mushrooms are usually more attractive in bright or earthy shades, smaller groupings often dress out well in colorful pastels or way-out color combinations of purples and hot pinks.

When considering the brightly colored, larger groupings, choosing the insect or animal that will be used as an accent piece will aid in determinating an overall color scheme. Remember that all stems and undersides of caps are to be creamy beige.

For the model used here, a miniature frog was chosen, his chartreuse (permanent green + cadmium yellow medium + white) and

The tiny frog's chartreuse and permanent green light dominate cap and stem markings in this mushroom grouping.

permanent green light colors dominating the cap and stem markings of the mushroom.

Using a #1 brush, outline the edge of the cap in chartreuse. Then, for a smooth finish use a #10 brush to fill in the cap's top. Paint *only* the top of the cap. Do *not* paint over the creamy-beige underside. Two coats will probably be necessary.

While the cap's second coat of chartreuse is drying, use a #000 brush and the same color to outline wishbone markings along the stem. As soon as all markings have been made, use a #000 brush and permanent green light to line each wishbone.

Move back to the caps and use this same brush and color (permanent green light) to outline five circles around the outer edge of each cap. If an insect or animal will not be perched on a cap, add several circles of varied size to its center portion. Fill in these circles, making spots of permanent green light. Use a second coat if the cap's chartreuse base coat shows through.

Next, while allowing these cap spots to dry, use a #000 brush to outline the outer edges of each wishbone stem marking in black. Since a thin outline is best, apply minimum pressure to the brush as you work.

When the wishbones are done, use the #000 brush to outline one half of each of the cap spots in black, being sure to choose the same half of all spots in a grouping. Start by applying light pressure at the top of each spot, exerting more pressure to thicken the line's middle portion, and lessening pressure as you reach the spot's lower half.

Flowers for this green-capped grouping may be of any bright color. Here each flower has four petals of cadmium orange and a brown center. Flowers should be randomly spaced in the modeling-paste grass.

When all painting has been completed, try various poses for the miniature frog (made, of course, according to instructions in the frog section). When you have chosen his resting spot, apply a dab of glue to each of his feet and press him gently but firmly into place.

Allow the arrangement to dry until the glue is almost clear. Then add your name or initials to one corner of the base rock, check the entire grouping for stray flecks of paint or other blemishes, and retouch where necessary. Remember, retouching that only takes a second or two helps to ensure the professional look which reflects the hours of work which have gone into the mushroom grouping. Apply the protective spray coating, following the directions in the "Spraying The Figures" section, only after all retouching has been done.

Base rocks of mushroom groupings are usually rough enough to warrant felting the arrangement's bottom to protect furniture and/or floors. For this final step, follow the felting instructions given for the owl.

The Antique Look. No creamy-beige coating is added to stems or caps for this third variation, and cap spots are first created by the use of modeling paste. These raised cap spots will take on contrasting hues when the antiquing layers are applied. Stem markings will be painted on later also.

Use a popsicle stick, palette knife, or brush to dab blobs of modeling paste onto the top of each cap. Apply five blobs to the outer portion of the cap's top, adding several additional blobs of varied size to the center portion if a cap will not have an insect or animal perched on it.

Now use a toothpick or the pointed wooden end of a #1 brush to make circular motions on each blob, creating the effect of a grained spot. These markings on the cap spots should probably start at the center and spiral outward.

After allowing the cap spots to dry overnight, proceed to the painting of stem markings.

First coat the stems and caps in tan gesso. When this gesso has dried thoroughly, use red oxide and black to make wishbone stem markings like those described for the natural-mushroom grouping. Next, don rubber gloves and proceed to antique the stems, caps, modeling-paste grass, and base rock according to the instructions given in the section "The Antiqued Owl."

When the antiquing has been completed, the raised cap spots should stand out because their grained areas have held more of the various colors than has the smoother surface around them. In composing a grouping with this style of mushroom, choose a rockcrafted accent animal or insect that blends well with the antiqued look of the rocks.

Remember to check the rockcrafted portions of your antiqued mushroom arrangement for stray flecks of paint or other blemishes before spraying on a protective satin-sheen finish according to the instructions under "Spraying The Figures" in Part I.

Whether your mushroom arrangement accents the natural color and texture of its rocks, highlights a room with its brightly colored caps, or exhibits the quieter beauty of an antiqued grouping, you can feel proud of having created one of the most difficult and challenging rockcrafting projects.

Part IV

ROCK PEOPLE OF DISTINCTION

Part IV

ROCK PEOPLE OF DISTINCTION

Once you have mastered the basic steps in rockcrafting animal figures, you will be able to create caricatures of people of any nationality or profession—from Indian to Eskimo, from nurse to fireman. Since you are limited by the rocks themselves, you may have trouble designing the man on stilts in the circus, but with a little imagination, even that project could be successful.

For people, as well as for insects and animals, the key word is caricature. If you want to manage an exact portrait of a neighbor's little boy, rockcrafting is the wrong medium. If you're content to caricature that boy in a baseball cap, striped polo shirt, and patched jeans, then put your creativity to work and glue and paint a rock boy.

To start you on the path to rockcrafted people of your own design, we have provided step-by-step instructions for four examples—Indian brave and maiden, a Chinese man, a geisha, and an Eskimo father, mother, and infant. Try them all, or make only one. Then, for the most rewarding kind of rockcrafting, apply the basic techniques to making figures you dream up yourself.

Indian

Indian brave, maiden, and tepee make an attractive grouping. Try one or both Indians, following the directions below, possibly adding special touches of your own. If you've already mastered the animals and insects described earlier, you should find this Indian grouping a relatively easy project.

Choosing The Rocks

Indian brave and maiden each require a round or oval body rock and a slightly smaller round or oval head rock. The head rock should be especially smooth to allow easier painting of facial features. Two oval foot rocks are needed; these should be approximately the shape of moccasins. You may wish to make the maiden slightly smaller than the brave.

A thin, elongated feather rock, slightly tapered at one end, is needed for the brave's headband. A large conical rock plus three sticklike pebbles will be used for the tepee for the Indian grouping. Perfect tepee rocks are hard to find, but any cylindrical rock in the right shape for the tepee's top can be broken off at a length and angle that will produce the desired effect. Sometimes natural forces have already broken the rock correctly, as in the case of the tepee in the photo.

Gluing the Rocks

Materials. The basic materials needed for gluing members of the Indian grouping are the same as those described under "Glue" in Part I. In addition, you will need a gluing frame and rubber bands like those described in the owl section. If you plan to construct brave and maiden at the same time, of course, you will need two frames.

Procedure. Gluing the head, body, and foot rocks is the same for brave and maiden. Get gluing frame, rubber bands, and props ready. Then place the two foot rocks on the bottom section of the frame so that the heels are almost together.

Next, put the body onto the foot rocks, letting the more rounded side form the front in order to achieve a pot-bellied look. Try putting the head into position before gluing feet to body to be sure that the rocks balance well and that either head or body rock will be in contact with the upright portion of the gluing frame. If space is left between head or body rock and the upright portion of the frame, check to be sure that space can be filled in with wood scraps and/or poker chips.

When you have determined the best positions for foot, head, and body rocks, apply a liberal dab of glue to each foot rock and press it firmly, but gently, into place. Crisscross the two rubber bands and secure over the nails shown in the photo of the owl construction, and then place any necessary chips between head and/or body rock and the upright portion of the gluing frame.

Allow the figure to dry on the gluing frame until the white glue turns clear. If the feet stick to the frame, slide a spatula between rocks and board to loosen the rocks.

The brave's feather rock will be glued on later, but the tepee rocks should be glued at this time. Two of the three rocks at the top of the tepee are placed at an angle, with the third rock almost upright between them. Apply a liberal dab of thick glue to the end of each small rock and press the rock into place, holding it until the glue sets well enough to allow the rock to remain in the chosen position.

Painting the Rocks

Materials. The Indian grouping requires the basic equipment described on pages 13-16, including #000, #1, and #10 red sable brushes. In addition to black and white acrylics, you will need yellow oxide and red oxide for skin tones and the buckskin suit and cadmium red light and permanent green light for beadwork and headband. The beadwork

An Indian brave, maiden, and tepee make an attractive grouping.

Rear View

Side View

and headband may, of course, be done in any bright colors of your own choosing. Raw sienna is needed for the tepee, plus bright colors for the tepee designs.

Procedure. Since Indian brave and maiden have identical suits of buckskin, you should probably paint both figures at once if you plan to make a grouping. Start by using a #10 brush to cover the feet with yellow oxide. Allow them to dry and use the #10 brush to paint the entire body with yellow oxide. Apply a second coat of yellow oxide when the first has dried.

Next, use a #1 or #000 brush and red oxide to paint the edge of the head rock where head and body meet. Then use a #10 brush to cover the entire remaining portion of the head in red oxide. Work for an especially smooth finish on the facial area. Make sure both red and yellow oxide are completely dry before proceeding with the next step.

Use a #000 brush to draw a black line all the way around the neck, which covers the glue joint between head and body rocks and forms the neckline of the buckskin suit. Then draw a black sleeve line from the front edge of the right shoulder about one-third of the way down the body rock. Then bring the line across horizontally toward the center front, ending about two-thirds of the way across toward the middle. Then draw a downward line, with a slight arc backward, to simulate the edge of the garment's cuff. Repeat for the left side.

Now add fringe lines along the right sleeve, starting at the cuff and moving to the point beneath the bend of elbow. Repeat for the left side. Then make a long fringe line at the center back of the suit, starting a bit below the neckline and ending about on a line with where the fringe on the sleeves ends. Apply more pressure at the top of this line and less at the bottom, so that the fringe ends in a narrow point. Add a line of fringe on either side of this middle one, making these two lines start a little lower than the center line and end a little above it, as shown in the sketch. Continue adding one line on each side until the fringe in the back meets the fringe on each sleeve.

Return to the front of the figure and use the #1 brush to outline a wrist and four chubby fingers for each arm. Then make a broken or dashed black line from center neckline to the base of the body rock. Form moccasin stitching by making a similar dashed line around each foot rock around the edge of the rock.

Fill in the hands with red oxide. Then use a #1 brush and black acrylic to draw on the hair. The hair of the maiden is parted and braided. Outline the right half of the head by drawing a line through the top of the head and a little to the right of center. Outline the forehead area of the right side of the hair, being careful to keep the hairline far enough back to give room for the eyes to be set relatively high on the face.

Outline the curved side and back portions of the hair and repeat the outlining procedure for the left side of the head, being careful to get the two sides as even as possible. Then fill in the outlines with black acrylic, using a #10 brush to achieve a smooth finish.

Turn the maiden so that her back is toward you and observe the right section of hair, noticing the point from which a braid would naturally originate—about midway along the base of the hair line. Begin the right braid at this point by making an outline similar to a pair of parentheses whose tops touch the hair line. Angle this first braid segment slightly toward the face as if coming over her shoulder, then add a second segment beneath the first and angle it a bit more. Add successive pairs, letting the braid grow at about a 45-degree angle until it ends at a point near the inside elbow of the buckskin suit. Avoid letting the braid obscure any of the shoulder or sleeve line.

Glue the feather rock so that its base rests just below the bottom portion of the headband.

Now fill in the braid with black and add a tassel of black hair at its end. Repeat this procedure for the left braid, being careful to match the two sides as to starting point, angle of fall, and length.

The brave's hair is shorter and features no braids. Using a #000 brush, outline a black circle, similar to a skull cap, on the top of the brave's head. Enlarge the circle to the desired size and shape for his hair. Making relatively long hair on the sides is a good idea, since this makes painting ears unnecessary. However, be sure to keep the hair in front high enough on the forehead to allow plenty of room for two large eyes.

Now, make thin brush strokes down toward the face all around to simulate hair. Again, keep the hair around the face short; you can lengthen it, if necessary, once you have completed the facial features.

Facial features are identical for brave and maiden, unless you prefer to omit the eyelashes for the brave. Use a #000 brush and black acrylic to outline two brows, a pair of oval eyes, two upcurved lashes, and an inverted "U" nose. You may choose to make a smiling mouth with laugh lines in the corners

or a dark oval mouth which seems to be exclaiming, "Oh!"

Fill in the eyes with white, using two or more coats. When the white paint has dried, outline two black pupils. These may be slightly crossed and looking up, or the brave may be looking at a shy maiden whose eyes are looking at the ground. Once the pupils have dried, superimpose a small dot of white on each of them to add sparkle to the eyes. When facial features have been completed, lengthen the brave's hair across the forehead, as necessary, styling as you go.

Use a #000 brush and cadmium red light to outline and fill in an oval band on the back of the Indian's head. While the band dries, use the #000 brush to make a single cadmium red light dot on each side of the first stitch mark of the line bisecting the front of the buckskin suit, one dot on the cuff area of each sleeve, and one dot on the toe of each moccasin. Paint two small bands of red at the end of each of the maiden's braids, just above the tassles of hair.

Now use the #000 brush and black acrylic to draw a series of slanted lines along the head band, alternating the direction of the lines, as shown in the photograph. Then use the #000 brush to place a dot of yellow oxide in the space between every other pair of lines. Finally, use the #000 brush to place a dot of permanent green light in each of the remaining spaces between the pairs of black lines.

Complete the beadwork on the buckskin suit and moccasins by placing three dots of permanent green light around each cadmium red light dot so that the green dots form the three points of a triangle, as can be seen in the photograph of the finished Indians earlier in this section.

The maiden is now completed, but the brave needs a feather for his headband. Apply one or two coats of black acrylic to the long flat feather rock. Then use a #000 brush to draw a white vein bisecting the rock. Starting at the narrower end of the rock, make pairs of slanted white lines along the central vein. Repeat this procedure for the other side of the feather.

Try positioning the feather so that its lower edge rests just below the bottom portion of the headband and note where the feather will touch the head rock. Apply a liberal dab of thick glue (see under "Gluing" in Part I on how to thicken the glue) to that part of the feather rock, and press the two rocks gently, but firmly, together. Hold the feather in place while you use your index finger or a toothpick to wipe off excess glue.

The tepee is painted next. Use a #10 brush to apply one or two coats of raw sienna to the main rock. Use a #1 brush to paint the three pebbles at the top a medium gray. Then use the #000 brush and black acrylic to outline a high, narrow rectangle on one side of the conical rock. Refer again to the picture of the finished Indians. To make the flap, draw a diagonal line from top left corner to bottom right corner. Fill in the left side of the rectangle with black acrylic.

Decorate the tepee's sides with Indian designs and/or symbols in bright colors. Use those in the photograph for models, or check an encyclopedia or book on Indian pictographs or designs.

When the tepee has been painted, you may wish to cover its bottom with felt, to avoid leaving a rough surface which might scratch floor or furniture. Cut a scrap of felt just smaller than the tepee's bottom, apply glue to the felt, and press it into place, smoothing out wrinkles.

Check tepee, brave, and maiden for blemishes and/or stray specks of paint, retouch where necessary, and spray on a protective satin-sheen finish, following directions and observing safety precautions given under "Spraying The Figures" in Part I.

Chinese Man

The Chinese man's sand dollar hat adds an unusual touch to this rockcrafted figure. Use him as an accent piece for book shelves or coffee table or to highlight a centerpiece when you're serving your favorite Chinese dish.

Choosing the Rocks

A round body rock, a slightly smaller round head rock, and two oval foot rocks are needed for the Chinese. Picking a smooth head rock will make painting facial features easier.

The Gluing

The basic materials and procedure for

gluing the head, body, and feet of the Chinese man are the same as those for the Indian in the preceding section.

The sand dollar hat, which will be glued on after all painting has been done, may be bought in a shell shop or picked up at the beach. If you get one at the beach, make sure the shell's inhabitant has left it and that the shell is smooth, not covered with rough, dark hairs.

This smiling Chinese man is ready for a coat of fixative.

Painting the Rocks

Materials. The Chinese man requires the basic painting equipment described under "Paints and Brushes" in Part I, including #000, #1, and #10 red sable brushes and gesso undercoating agent. In addition to black and white acrylics, you will need Oriental yellow (cadmium yellow medium + yellow oxide) for his face and hands and a bright color for his shirt.

In this case, chartreuse (cadmium yellow + permanent green light + white) was used, but bright blue (phtalocyanine blue + white), burnt orange (cadmium orange + cadmium red light), bright green (permanent green light), rose pink (acra violet + white), or cadmium red light would all be good choices for shirt colors. Avoid any yellows or golds that are too close to the color of the hands and face.

Procedure. Use a #10 brush to apply a coat of gesso to all parts of the figure except the bottoms of his feet. Using a #1 brush, begin the black trousers by carefully edging the bottom of the body rock where it meets the feet. Then use a #10 brush to paint the lower two-thirds of the body rock black. Though the bright shirt will cover the top two-thirds of the rock, you don't want to risk having the edge of the pants too low.

To prevent leaving an obvious line where the black paint ends, clean your brush lightly over the edge where the black paint stops. As the black thins out onto the gesso, the possibility of leaving a sharp ridge which would be obvious under the bright shirt is eliminated.

When the pants have been completed, use a #1 brush and a mixture of cadmium yellow medium and yellow oxide to paint the bottom area of the head rock where head meets body. Then paint the neck joint itself, plus a little line of yellow around the top of the body rock, since it is an open-necked shirt. Now use a #10 to completely cover the head rock. When this yellow paint has dried, use the #10 brush to apply a second coat to the face and neck area.

Now paint the bright jacket, using any of the colors suggested earlier. Start by painting a neckline with a #1 brush, beginning at center back and edging the neckline all the way around to center front, where you should leave a small "V" of flesh exposed at the collar line.

Continue the shirt by covering the top two-thirds of the body rock, applying a second coat when the first one has dried. To be sure the top of the black trousers is well covered, use a third and fourth coat in this area, if necessary.

Use a #10 or #000 brush to paint the tops of the feet white, being careful not to get white paint onto the bottom edges of the black trousers. Apply second and third coats, if necessary.

Now use a #1 brush to edge the sandal in black, letting the black come up high enough on the edges of the foot rocks to make the black portion clearly visible from the top. Then cover the bottoms of the feet in black. To complete the sandals, use a #000 brush to paint crossed straps on the top of each foot, making the broad "X" a quarter to a third of the way from toe to ankle area.

Move now to the hair of the Chinese, and use a #1 or #000 brush to sketch his hairline. His basic style features a deeply parted center section and a single pigtail or queue. Begin by making a pair of deep curves which start high at the center front of the forehead. Continue the two curves around the two sides of the head, bringing them low enough on each side to avoid the necessity of painting ears and letting them meet low on the back of the head rock. Now use a #10 brush to fill in the outline with black.

Next, outline a pair of parentheses which seem to hang from the lowest point at the center back of the hairline. Add a second pair suspended from the first, than a third, keeping the queue on the shirt and stopping the additions soon enough to allow room for a tassel to be drawn at the bottom of the braid. Now fill in the parentheses, thus completing the hair style.

Move to the shirt next, using a #000 brush to outline the entire top edge of the shirt in black, following the line where shirt color meets the yellow of the neck. Continue this outlining process by edging the "V" at the neckline in black. Then bring down a narrow black line from the point of the "V" to the top of the pants.

Next, turn the figure so his left side is facing you and begin a sleeve line which angles back toward the hips and continues about half-way down the chartreuse jacket. Add a horizontal line which begins just above the spot where the slanting line ends and continues to a point about two-fifths of the way across the front portion of the body rock. Complete the sleeve by drawing a vertical cuff line from the end of the horizontal line down to the top of the pants. Repeat for the other sleeve.

Using a #000 and black acrylic, outline a pair of clasped hands in the area between the two cuffs. Disregard the black line which the mitten-shaped hands must cover, since the two coats of yellow skin tone, which should now be applied, will hide the line.

When the skin tone has dried, use a #000 and thin black acrylic to sharpen the hand outlines. Then make the small brocade frog fastener at the top of the shirt, just below the "V."

Now use a #000 brush and black acrylic to make an inverted "V" slit at the bottom edge of the shirt, just under the elbow area. Fill in the slit with black and repeat for the other side. Make a similar inverted "V" slit at the center front of the shirt.

Use a #000 and thin black acrylic to paint the facial features, including arched brows, slanted eyes, a "U" nose, and a broad, upcurved mouth with a single smile line in each corner.

The Chinese man is now ready for his sand dollar hat. Shake as much sand as possible from the center hole of the sand dollar. Then, since treated sand dollars purchased in hobby or shell shops tend to be quite soft, you might consider reinforcing the hat with a *thin* layer of glue. Apply the glue with your index finger, completely covering all parts of the sand dollar. Within a few minutes, the glue will begin to dry clear, letting the sand dollar's characteristic pattern stand out.

If you prefer to reinforce the hat by applying a coat of acrylic, raw sienna is a good color choice, but remember, the paint will most likely obscure the sand dollar's natural texture and design.

When the hat has been reinforced by one of these methods, try positioning it on the head of the figure, tilting it slightly backward to avoid hiding the facial features. Now apply a dab of thick glue to the hole in the sand dollar's underside; this helps keep sand from leaking out. Next, apply a circle of glue ½ inch in diameter to the underside of the sand dollar's center. Then press the sand dollar firmly, but gently, into place on the head rock.

Because of the slight angle at which it is set, the hat tends to slip off if not propped. A few wood scraps and poker chips placed under its back edge will serve to hold it until the blob of glue dries clear.

Check the finished figure for stray specks of paint and/or other blemishes, retouching where necessary, and spray on a protective plastic finish, following the instructions and observing the safety precautions given under "Spraying The Figures" in Part I.

Don't be dismayed to find that a natural-finish sand dollar (or even one you've reinforced with a thin coat of glue) is too absorbent to take on a satin-sheen finish. Since even multiple coats of fixative will not give the hat a shiny surface, let a single coat suffice. Anyway, it would be too bad to destroy the sand dollar's natural finish, which adds a striking touch to the finished Chinese figure.

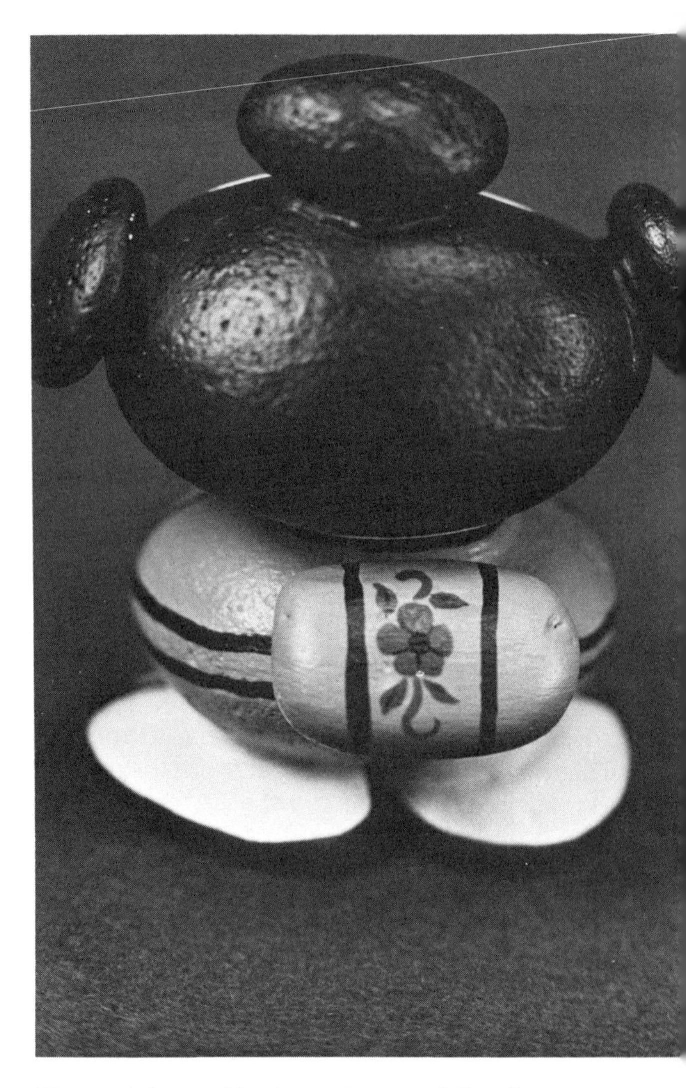

The geisha, with her characteristic flowers-decorated obi.

Geisha

A geisha, or Japanese dancing girl, makes an especially attractive accent piece in homes with oriental decor. Also quite impressive as the focal point for a centerpiece designed to complement a Japanese menu, the geisha can be created by following these relatively simple steps.

Choosing the Rocks

Just as for the Indian figures, a round body rock, a slightly smaller round head rock, and two oval foot rocks are needed for the geisha. The head rock should be especially smooth, to allow for easier painting of facial features.

In addition to these basic rocks, three small, button-shaped rocks of medium thickness and similar size are needed for the geisha's hair, and a square or rectangular rock of medium thickness for the large rear portion of her obi (the sash worn around her waist). Look at the rear-view photo of the finished geisha to get an idea of the correct size for the obi rock.

Gluing the Rocks

Materials. The basic materials for gluing the geisha are the same as those described under "Glue" in Part I. In addition, you will need a gluing frame and rubber bands like those described in the owl section.

Procedure. For gluing the geisha, go by the steps for putting together the rocks for the Indian figures. After this first gluing session, allow the head, body, and foot rocks to dry on the frame until the white glue has turned clear. Then remove the geisha from the frame, using a spatula, if necessary, to loosen the rocks from the wood.

The second gluing session begins with placement of the three hair rocks. Try positioning the button-shaped rocks on the geisha's head, putting one in the center-front portion of her crown and one on each side of her head. When satisfied with this positioning, apply a generous dab of *thick* glue to the central hair rock and press the rock gently, but firmly, into place, holding it there until danger of slipping seems past.

Now, with wood scraps and chips ready, apply a generous dab of *thick* glue to the right hair rock, press the rock into place, and prop with wood scraps and/or chips. Repeat for the left hair rock.

Being careful not to disturb the newly propped hair pieces, turn the gluing board around so the geisha faces away from you. Now place the obi rock over the small of the back, in approximately the position of a bow on a little girl's sash. If your rock is rectangular, place it lengthwise across the back.

With props ready, apply a generous dab of *thick* glue to the obi rock, press into place, and prop it with wood scraps and/or chips. After the second gluing session, again leave the geisha to dry until the white glue turns clear.

Painting

Materials. Painting the geisha requires the use of the basic painting equipment described under "Paints and Brushes" in Part I, including #000, #1, and #10 red sable brushes and the gesso undercoating agent. In addition to black and white acrylics, you will need a bright color for the kimono, a second color for its decorative flowers, plus permanent green light for flower leaves and stems. Cadmium red light and phtalocyanine blue make a good combination for the kimono and flowers, so we'll mention those colors in giving instructions.

Procedure. Before applying any acrylics, use a #10 brush to give a smooth coating of gesso to the entire geisha, except for the bottoms of her feet. Then use a #1 brush and cadmium red light to paint the kimono. Begin by outlining the top of the garment, leaving a small area of gesso, since the kimono's neckline should be fairly low.

Next, skip to the bottom edge of the body rock, where body and tops of feet meet. Work carefully here to avoid smearing red paint onto the foot rocks. When top and bottom portions of the kimono have been edged in red, switch to a #10 brush and cover the kimono area, working to achieve a smooth finish. Apply a second coat of red when the first has dried.

Move to the head rock next, using a #1 brush and white acrylic to cover the exposed area of the body rock just above the kimono's neckline, the glue joint between head and body rocks, and the bottom portion of the head rock. Then switch to a #10 brush and cover the entire head rock, minus the three hair rocks. Work to achieve an especially

The completed geisha, with hairdo, makeup, kimono, and sandals.

smooth finish on face and neck, applying a second and even a third coat to these areas if necessary.

The geisha's hair is painted next. Using a #1 or #000 brush, make a marked widow's peak in the center of the forehead, bringing the brush up on the right side to form a high curve which ends in a second, narrower peak on that side. Move from this second peak to a shallow curve which moves down and back around the side of the rock, stopping at center back. Repeat for the left side, letting the two lines meet in the back. Fill in the hair area with black, being especially careful to cover completely the balls of hair and the joints where the balls are glued to the head.

When the hair has been completed, use a #1 or a #000 brush and white acrylic to paint the tops of the foot rocks, being careful to avoid getting white paint onto the red kimono.

Next, use a #1 brush to edge the sandals in black, letting the black come up high enough on the edges of the foot rocks to make the black edging clearly visible from the top. Then cover the bottoms of the feet in black. To complete the sandals, use a #000 brush to paint a single strap across the toe area, as shown in the photo.

Next, move to the detail work on the kimono, starting by using a #000 brush to edge the collar in black. Then draw a shoulder seam which starts at the collar edge a bit toward the front of the left shoulder's center and extends to the bottom of the body rock. Now outline the top of the sleeve by painting a horizontal line which begins at a point one-third of the way down the right shoulder line and extends all the way across the front of the kimono, ending at the opposite shoulder line.

Next, complete the sleeves by drawing a vertical line which starts at the center of the horizontal sleeve line and bisects the lower two-thirds of the kimono, ending at the bottom of the body rock. Make a dashed line of topstitching on either side of this solid one, indicating the hems of the two sleeves. The long, full sleeves, of course, hide the clasped hands.

A slanted line beginning at the center of the neckline and ending on the horizontal sleeve line at a point slightly to the left of center represents the kimono's wrap-around opening.

Now, turn the geisha so that her right side is facing you. Using a #000 brush and thin acrylic, outline the sash by starting a line under the edge of the obi rock and bringing it straight across to the shoulder line. Draw a second line parallel to the first and about ¼ inch below it, or what looks best on the size rocks you're working on. Repeat, making identical parallel lines on the other side of the body rock.

Next, turn the geisha so that the obi rock faces you and use a #000 brush and thin black acrylic to draw a vertical line from top to bottom of the obi rock a quarter of the way from the rock's right edge. Draw a second vertical line an equal distance from the obi rock's left edge.

In the center portion of the obi rock, paint a single flower of phthalocyanine blue. Lay the end of a #000 brush flat against the rock to form five petals radiating from a center point. While this flower dries, make a similar blossom on each sleeve, just outside the dashed hem line of each cuff.

Return to the obi flower and use a #000 brush and green to draw curved stem lines above and below the flower. Add two tiny leaves to each stem line. Then add stem and leaves to the top of the flowers on the sleeves.

Again using a #000 brush and thin black acrylic, draw lines separating the five segments of the obi and sleeve flowers and lines bisecting each leaf. Then add a black dot in each flower's center.

Proceed to the facial features, using a #000 brush and thin black acrylic to draw arched brows, slanted eyes, a "U" nose, and upturned mouth with a single smile line in each corner.

The geisha's makeup, which drastically alters this simple Oriental face, should be applied with great care, since crimson red errors are not easily eradicated from a chalk-white face. First, use the #000 brush to outline a pair of crimson red rouge spots, being careful to make the spots at equal distance from the nose and as identical in size and shape as possible. Then apply crimson red "lipstick" to form a generous pair of pursed lips bisected by the smiling mouth line.

When the geisha has been painted, make a check of the kimono to see whether you need to even up the black lines by patching here and there with cadmium red light. Since leaving wobbly, uneven lines can spoil the effect you've worked so hard to create, don't skip this important retouching step.

Finally, examine the geisha for other blemishes, retouch where necessary, and apply a protective satin-sheen finish. Since crimson red tends to run if sprayed too heavily, apply only a single, light coat of fixative to the geisha's face.

Eskimo

A rockcrafted Eskimo mother, father, and child standing by a rock igloo make a striking group. Though the figures look relatively complicated, they are not difficult if made according to the following step-by-step directions.

Choosing the Rocks

The Eskimo father's body rock, a relatively flat oval of medium thickness, is similar to a thick turtle body rock. The Eskimo head rock is a smaller rock of similar shape, color, and texture. Two small, round mitten rocks are also required. Matching head, body, and mitten rocks will allow you to let the natural surface of the rocks provide the desired roughened-leather look for parka and mittens. Remember that wetting the rocks before comparing them ensures a better match, since the spray fixative will permanently darken the finished figure in much the same way that water temporarily darkens the rocks. The two oval foot rocks will be painted, so they need not be matched in color or texture.

The rocks for the Eskimo woman are similar to those needed for the man, though the woman in a matched pair is usually smaller. For the one-rock cradleboard and baby, choose an elongated flat rock slightly larger at one end than the other. Since this rock's size depends on the size of the parents, you might wish to wait until you have glued and painted the mother to choose the rock for the baby.

The igloo is made of a rock in the shape of half a sphere. Rock hemispheres are fairly common, but you may need to break a round rock or find one broken in two by natural forces. The entrance tunnel will be represented by an oval painted on the dome.

The igloo grouping is ready to receive a single coat of satin-sheen fixative.

Gluing the Rocks

Materials. The basic materials needed for gluing the Eskimo are the same as those listed under "Glue" in Part I. In addition, you will need a gluing frame and rubber bands like the set described in the owl section. If you are gluing the man and woman at once, you'll need to construct two of these frames.

You will also need fur or a synthetic fur fabric for trimming the parka, boots, mittens, and cradleboard. Hobby shops often have imitation fur, but the type found in fabric centers is usually more like that used on Eskimo parkas in the north. Another source of fur would be discarded coats, muffs, or collars. One full-length coat has provided many Daystone Eskimos with fur that adds richness to the finished figure. Of course, you'll want to limit your scavenging to muff or collar, unless you're planning to produce quite a few Eskimos! A damp cloth for cleaning fingers while working with glue and fur will save your nerves and ensure a neater gluing job. Scissors will be needed for trimming the fur.

Procedure. Get the gluing frame, rubber bands, and props ready. Then place the two foot rocks on the bottom section of the frame so that the heels are almost together. Then put the body onto the foot rocks, letting the flatter side form the front of the Eskimo.

Try positioning the head rock with its more rounded side forming the Eskimo's face. Be sure the head and body are well balanced so the finished figure will not be tipsy. Since either head or body rock should be in contact with the upright portion of the gluing frame, you may need to insert one or more chips behind head or body rock to achieve the correct positioning. When satisfied, apply a liberal dab of glue to the foot rocks, and press the body rock firmly, but gently, into place.

Apply a generous dab of glue to the head rock and press it into place on the body rock. Crisscross two rubber bands and hook into place on the nails. Place any necessary chips between head and/or body rocks and the upright portion of the gluing frame. You may need to use a third rubber band around the figure's middle to hold it against the back of the frame. Use your index finger to wipe off excess glue around the neck area now, since the Eskimo's head may be easily dislodged if you exert too much pressure while trimming dried glue from this area.

The mitten rocks and the fur trim on the Eskimo's parka, boots, and mittens will be glued after painting has been completed. For now, allow the Eskimo to dry on the gluing frame until the white glue turns clear. If the feet stick to the frame, slide a spatula between rocks and board to loosen the rocks.

Painting

The Eskimo man and wife are painted identically, so doing both adults at once saves time if you are making a grouping.

Unless a large, unsightly blob of glue has run down onto body rock or feet, there is no need for trimming, since joints will be covered with fur. In fact, leaving the jointed areas untrimmed can ensure a longer-lasting Eskimo, while exerting excess pressure with a razor blade can easily snap head and body rocks apart.

Materials. The Eskimo grouping requires the basic materials described under "Paints and Brushes" in Part I, including #000, #1, and #10 red sable brushes. In addition to black and white acrylics, you will need burnt sienna and raw sienna for the Eskimos and phthalocyanine blue for the igloo.

To complete the figures, you'll need the fur pieces, scissors, glue, and damp cloth described earlier in this section.

Procedure—Mother, Father, and Baby. Begin the adult Eskimo by using a #000 brush to apply raw sienna to the top edges of the feet, being careful not to get paint onto the body rock. Then use a #10 brush to finish covering the feet.

A mixture of burnt sienna and white is needed for the Eskimo's flesh color. If you're making a family, be sure to mix enough paint to have plenty left for the baby's face. Cover the paint tightly so it won't dry out before you need it.

First, use a #1 brush to outline the facial area of the head rock. Think of the rock as a hamburger bun standing on end and draw the face line along the bun's slice line. Don't go farther back than this point or you'll get paint onto the unpainted part of the head rock, which will represent the rough leather of the parka hood. Next, achieve a smooth finish by filling in the outline with a #10 brush. Apply a second coat, again using a #10 brush.

Use a #000 brush to add black hair around the Eskimo's face. Starting at the center of the forehead, lay the brush, tip forward, along the flesh line to form jagged bangs. Work from the forehead's center halfway down the right side of the face. Repeat for the left side. Be careful not to get the bangs much beyond the flesh line around the front edges, since you want to leave plenty of room for facial features. Also, keep the smooth edge of the hair even with the flesh line to avoid getting black paint onto the natural rock which will become the leather of the parka hood.

Create facial features by using a #000 brush and thin black acrylic to outline brows, slanted eyes, a "U" nose, and an up-curving mouth with a single smile line at each corner. When the facial features are completed, lengthen the bangs, if necessary.

The mother and father receive one final bit of painting—a row of three "X"'s down the center of each boot. Use the #000 brush and thin black acrylic to create these laces.

Note that the skin tone is applied only to the front half *of the head rock.*

Now that the painting steps have been completed, the Eskimo should be dressed in bits of fur. Be sure the figure has dried completely before beginning the fur trimming, for the pressure required when gluing on fur is often great enough to cause heads or feet to snap away from the body rock if the glue has not set well.

Begin by measuring and cutting all strips that will be used on the Eskimo. First, cut a strip ⅝ of an inch wide of your richest-looking fur scrap. This will become the parka hood, the focal point of the finished figure. The length of this strip will depend on the size of the head rock. To determine that length, first examine the fur to see where your best area begins. If this choice area begins at one end of the strip, place the edge of that end flush against the neck joint and hold it in place. Then stretch the fur around the edge of the head rock, just back of the hairline. Push the fur into the neck area on the other side, estimating where the strip must be cut in order for the fur on that side to be flush with the neck joint.

If the best-looking section of your fur is in the middle of the strip, then you'll need to place the richest portion on top of the

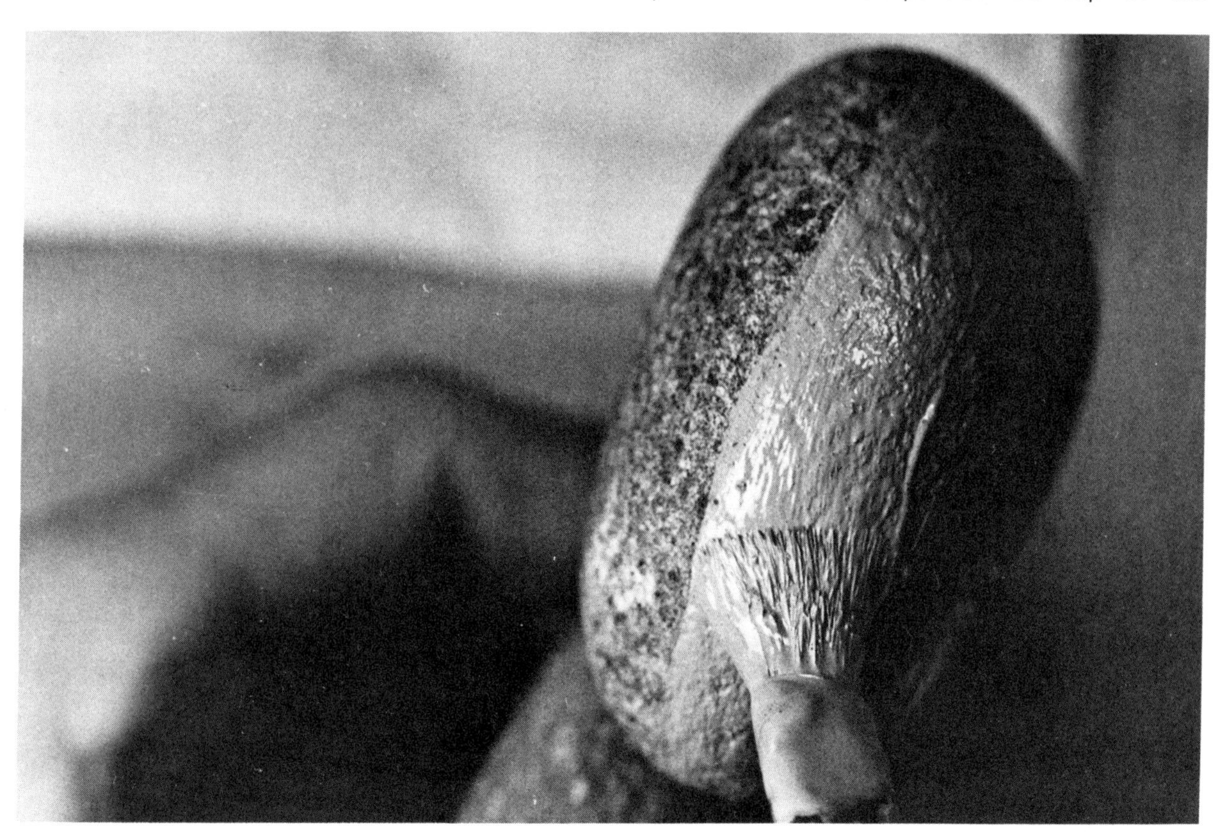

Eskimo's head and stretch the two ends down to the neck area, using your thumbs to press the fur in at the neck joint so you can estimate where it should be cut.

The neck piece is cut next. This strip, trimmed to about a ½-inch width, should be placed around the neck, pulled tight in the center front, then cut to a length just long enough to encircle the neck with the two ends being glued flush with one another. Trim sharp corners of the cut ends to insure a snug fit in the neck area.

Fur for the bottom edge of the parka is cut next. Use a piece ⅝ of an inch wide, pulling it tight so that it meets in the center front of the body rock, two-thirds of the way down the rock. Cut this piece so that the ends will just stretch to meet, flush with each other. Check to be sure the two ends are equal in width. If not, even them up with the scissors.

The two boots require a single length of fur 5/16 of an inch wide. Fur cut any narrower usually pulls apart when you stretch it. Start the measuring by pressing one end of the strip into the area between the two feet. Hold it there while you wrap fur around one foot, press it into the area between the two feet in back, and bring it around the other foot to end in front again, between the feet. Cut off excess fur at this point.

When the fur for parka and boots has been measured and cut, check to be sure you have pulled off any loose fur that might still be clinging to the strips after your trimming has been completed.

Glue the pieces in the order in which they were cut, starting with the parka hood. Use your index finger to apply glue to the skin side of the fur strip, being especially careful to cover the edges and ends of the strips well. CAUTION: Use the damp cloth to wipe all glue from your fingers after each application.

Then, press the center of the strip into place on the top of the head rock, just back of the hairline. Now, bring your fingers on around both sides of the head rock, pressing the fur into place as you go. Finally, press the ends into place against the neck joint. Repeat this pressing procedure again, starting at the top of the head and working around to the neck joint to push out any wrinkles or air bubbles.

Attach the collar piece in much the same way, this time starting at the center back of the neck and bringing the fur around both sides so that it meets at center front. The edges of fur of the parka hood should be *under* the fur collar piece. Be sure to pull the fur very tight, trimming again, if necessary. Press firmly, but gently, using the tips of your nails to push the glued side of the fur into the narrow joint where body and neck meet. Rough handling can cause even a well-dried glue job to fail.

To attach the fur that goes around the bottom of the jacket, apply glue to the skin side and lay the strip, glue side up, on the table. Then lay the Eskimo on its back on the strip of fur so that the glued strip touches the body rock about two-thirds of the way down the rock. Bring the fur forward, around both sides, so that its two edges meet flush in the center front of the body rock. Pick the Eskimo up and press firmly, but gently, all the way around the fur piece.

Apply glue to the smooth side of the boot fur strip, press the center of the glue-lined strip between the two feet in back, using a fingernail or the wooden tip of a paintbrush to make sure the strip fits down between the feet well. Then, holding this spot in place, pull the strip around the right foot, tucking one edge into the front space between the two feet. Repeat for the left side, being sure the two ends meet in the space between the feet. Press the strip into place all around the feet.

The mitten rocks are glued on at this time. The two rocks, touching or nearly touching, fit in the open area between fur collar and fur bottom of the parka jacket. After figuring out the best position for them, apply a generous blob of *thick* glue to each one, and use your thumbs to press them into place. Hold them there for a few minutes if they seem apt to slide out of place.

Now cut about a 2″ × 3″ scrap of fur and place a 2-inch end against the top, outside portion of one mitten rock, measuring to determine the width needed to cover that edge of the rock, and the length needed to form the cuff and sleeve which cover the top half of the rock and extend onto the edge of the shoulder. Be sure to cut the piece large enough, since you can always trim excess but cannot add needed width or length. When you have estimated the width, cut a U-shaped piece of fur out of one end of the 2″ × 3″ scrap. This piece, shaped like a rounded shirt pocket, will be placed so that the straight edge goes over the hand area of the mitten rock and the rounded edge covers the back of the rock toward the shoulder. Using, the first sleeve as a model (but taking into account possible size and shape differences in the two mitten rocks), cut a second piece for the other sleeve. Remember that most fur has a nap and you must cut the two pieces so that the finished sleeves will match. Cut them so that the nap lies forward over the exposed mitten rock, thus hiding the raw edge of the fur strip.

Apply glue to the skin side of the sleeve fur and press the fur gently, but firmly, into place, remembering that the glue holding the mitten rock has not yet had time to dry. Repeat for the second mitten.

If you're making an Eskimo family grouping, you will need to choose a rock for the baby and cradleboard as soon as you've finished attaching the fur to the mother Eskimo's mittens. If you've set aside one or two possible baby rocks, try each one for size at this time by placing the rock against the mother's back so that the wider end rests against the fur at the bottom of her parka and the narrower end extends over her left shoulder far enough to allow the baby's face to be seen. Usually about half the rock should extend over the shoulder.

When you have chosen the best rock for this particular mother, place it against the mother's back once more, this time to ascertain just where the face should be painted. Now use a #1 brush to paint the whole face in the same flesh color used for the parents (burnt sienna + white), making an outline approximately the shape of a thumbnail. Apply a second coat, using a #10 brush to achieve a smooth finish.

Use a #000 brush and thin black acrylic to make wisps of hair around the baby's face. Start at the center of the forehead and work around the face to the lower edges of the sides. Keep the hairline high enough to allow plenty of room for facial features.

Use a #000 brush and thin black acrylic to paint on facial features, making the child's face a miniature version of his mother's. If you wish to lengthen his bangs, do so at this time.

Cut a rectangle of fur just larger than the baby rock and curve the corners slightly. Try

Mother, father, and child from the back showing their leather and fur parkas and boots.

placing the baby's back against the smooth side of the fur and pulling the fur up so the entire back and sides of the rock are covered with fur.

When satisfied with the fit, apply glue to the smooth side of the fur, being sure to get all edges covered. Remember to wipe excess glue from your fingers with the damp cloth before proceeding. You don't want fur all stuck together in spots with glue. Now, place the back of the rock against the glued side of the fur and pull the fur up around the face and body, pressing the fur into place.

Finally, apply a liberal blob of thick glue to the bare tummy area of the baby, smoothing the glue over all the area that will touch the mother's back. Press the baby firmly, but gently, into place and hold him there for a minute until it seems secure. Then lay the mother on her back to dry, propping if necessary.

Procedure—The Igloo. The igloo is the final item in the Eskimo grouping. First use a #10 brush to cover the bottom of the dome in igloo white (titanium white + trace of black + trace of phthalocyanine blue). Allow the bottom to dry, then set the igloo upright and apply a coat of white to the remaining portion of the rock. Apply a second coat to the dome, and a third, if necessary. Since the bottom will be covered with felt, it needs no second coat.

When the white paint has dried, use a #1 brush and black acrylic to outline an arched entranceway. The top of the arch should be about halfway between the igloo's base and top. Fill in the entranceway, using a #10 brush to create a smooth, black surface.

Start the igloo blocks at the bottom right, using a #1 brush and black acrylic to draw a single row of blocks, extending from the right side of the doorway all the way around to the left side. Draw each block separately, rounding its corners slightly, since simply drawing a line around the bottom and marking off segments results in an igloo that looks like a prefab job!

Make a second row of blocks, arranging them so that their seam lines fall in the middle of the blocks of the first row. Continue making rows in this way until you near the top of the dome. At that point you will need to work the blocks into the arrangement that seems most logical, in view of the small area available. Our model features a top made of three central blocks.

When the blocks have been completed, cut a piece of felt a fraction smaller than the bottom of the dome. Spread a thin layer of glue on the felt and press it into place on the bottom of the igloo.

All figures for the Eskimo grouping should be checked for stray specks of paint and/or other blemishes, retouched wherever necessary, and given a protective satin-sheen finish. Be careful not to spray the fur too heavily. Remember, also, that the unpainted areas of mittens, head, and body will lose their natural look if sprayed too heavily.

Once you've made one of the human figures described in the preceding pages, you should have mastered the basic techniques

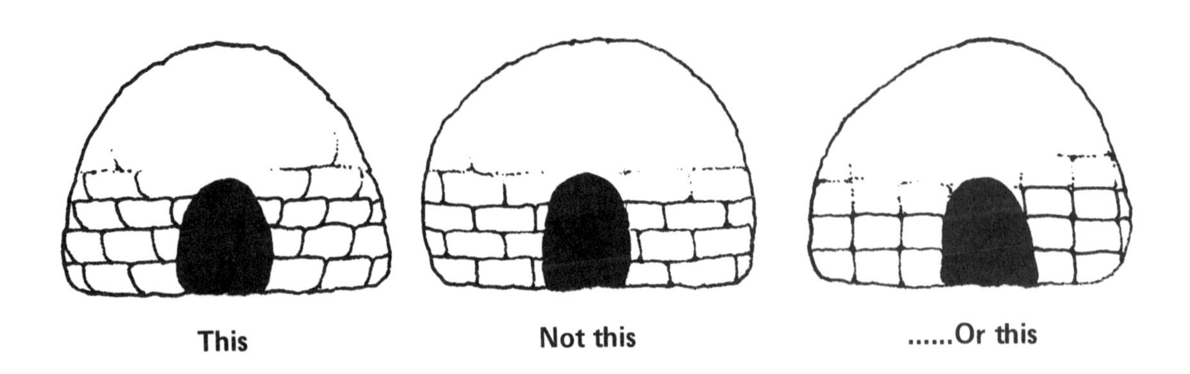

This **Not this** **......Or this**

involved in caricaturing rock people. Try more of our models, or proceed with ideas of your own. The sizes and shapes of available rocks and the extent of your own ingenuity will determine the artistic success of your original endeavors, but with a little practice you should be able to design and create pieces for every occasion.

Be brave! Try making special people rocks for that next office party or the Little League awards banquet. You'll enjoy the challenge, and your rockcrafted favors are sure to bring amusement and delight, maybe even a little praise.

Part V

PUTTING IT ALL TO USE

Part V

PUTTING IT ALL TO USE

Now that you've not only mastered the basic skills of rockcrafting but have also advanced to such complicated items as bears, owls, and people, you should be anxious to display your creations. Be bold! Let your rockcrafted items become integral parts of your decorating and entertaining plans. The pictures and suggestions on the following pages indicate a few of the many ways rockcrafted items may be used, but are intended primarily to trigger your imaginatgion

Two mallards displayed on shelves made from discarded items found at an abandoned silver mill.

in making the most of your original creations.

The simplest way to display a rockcrafted item is to use it as you would use any other ornamental object—by displaying it on shelves or coffee tables. The wooden shelves shown here were found at an abandoned silver mill, but you could fashion similar shelves from scraps of weathered wood and two pieces of ¾-inch plywood cut into half circles. Put up on a brick wall, the shelf is ideal for displaying these two mallards.

A tiny mallard adorns the top of a wrought-iron matchbox holder in Jere's house, and two yellow ducklings on the yellow kitchen wall phone amuse her while someone's keeping her on "hold."

The rockcrafted fish here share their home with starfish and pieces of coral. Appropriately, the shelf hangs on a bathroom wall. Placing any rockcrafted fish or water fowl on a bathroom shelf adds a welcome decorative touch.

End-table and buffet arrangements can be reflections of changing moods or seasons.

These rockcrafted fish share their wicker shelf with starfish and pieces of coral.

A simple piece of driftwood becomes an eyecatching buffet piece when two rockcrafted owls are placed beside it. Notice the complementary textures of the pieces.

A large rockcrafted item, such as a mallard, often adds charm to the hearthside scene. If a doorstop is called for, why not use a cheerful one, such as a giant turtle whose shell features a design of your own that complements the color scheme of the room whose door it holds open.

Sometimes, like an excellent piece of sculpture, large rockcrafted items are striking enough to stand alone, to be appreciated for their beauty or uniqueness, not for any utilitarian reason. One such piece, the pelican shown here, is highly prized by their owners and highly praised by visitors.

Some really large items, like Herniatia, the Day's lawn duck, seem best suited for use out of doors. A giant frog can add a cheery touch to a fountain or fish pond. Or try natural-rock mushrooms in a flowerbed, where they're so real-looking your friends will be doing double-takes.

Even smaller items, such as a flower-bed chipmunk perched on driftwood, can be used

A piece of driftwood and two owls make a simple but impressive buffet piece.

This brown pelican, specially ordered as a memento of a Florida visit, is an conversation piece.

This large frog guards a backyard goldfish pond.

A brown and white rock chipmunk hides among pink daisies.

outside. Or a tiny turtle on a tree trunk. Just remember to apply adequate coatings of fixative to all glued areas of any pieces which will be exposed to the temperature and humidity extremes of outdoor settings.

When cold weather strikes and outdoor flowers fade, try brightening the house with arrangements which feature rock creatures. Let a turtle peek from among potted daisies. Use a geisha or Chinese man with an Oriental arrangement. Place a frog in a hanging pot of ivy. Glue a ladybug to a leaf and create an arrangement to delight a friend in the hospital.

With the terrarium's increasing popularity, tiny rockcrafted figures are in greater and greater demand. Place a miniature turtle in among the tiny plants. Fashion a frog to hide behind a fern. Let a ladybug explore a broad leaf.

Using rockcrafted items in these ways calls for no special adaptations of the items for which we've already given instructions, but slight modifications are advised if you plan to use rock items as wall hangings. The basic key to the creation of a wall hanging is to make the item as flat as possible. Then use thick glue to secure a wire loop to its backside. Try twisting the wire to make a loop on each end. Then fill the bottom loop with glue and let the top one serve as a hanger. Be sure to let the glue dry until it is completely clear and to test the hook's strength carefully before hanging the item up.

Make a hanging elephant for the nursery wall or design tropical fish to match a bathroom color scheme. Try hanging a group of owls made of rocks plus modeling paste and finished by the antiquing process described in the owl section.

Single rocks can be painted with flowers and/or insects or even a miniature landscape. Let your imagination lead you to new ways of creating rockcrafted wall hangings for your home or that of a friend.

Carrying out a holiday theme with rockcrafted items gives your dinner party that special touch which makes it an event to re-

Most perplexed, this miniature owl, made from a small flat rock, features rock eyes and beak, modeling-paste feathers, and an antiqued finish.

These flat, oval rocks feature painted flowers, mushrooms, and a snail.

Beard and fur trim of modeling paste highlight this eleven-rock Santa.

member. Try a Halloween centerpiece which features owls and pumpkins. You might even wish to make the pumpkins themselves from rocks. An Indian brave, maiden, and tepee, plus dried grasses, make Thanksgiving dinner doubly special, and a rock Santa plus bits of holly can add an original touch to the traditional Christmas feast.

Special nonholiday occasions call for originality, too. How about cooling off a summer party by seating guests at a table draped in a snow-white cloth and featuring an Eskimo family, complete with igloo? Refreshments? Baked Alaska, of course.

Ladybugs on mushrooms make a bright centerpiece for a spring luncheon, and ladybug placecards become take-home favors for guests. The earthy colors of an antiqued owl are the perfect answer to the need for an autumn luncheon's centerpiece. Make a wedding shower an event to remember by creating a tiny favor for each—a pastel turtle carrying an umbrella painted in flowers and colors to match her own.

Need party decorations for a really out-of-the-ordinary occasion? Put on your thinking cap and you'll soon come up with ideas that start new ideas popping so fast you'll end up with so many you can't use them all. Jere once had the assignment of creating a centerpiece for a most unlikely occasion—a park ranger's retirement banquet. She simply put a ranger

Ladybug placecards become favors for guests.

A lazy bear in an appropriate hat highlights a park ranger's retirement banquet.

With the wide variety of hats available from hobby shops and novelty outlets, a rockcrafter should be able to create a unique figure for most any occasion.

hat on a lazy bear and surrounded the bear with colorful maps and brochures from the park. The ranger hat, like the hats in the photo, was obtained from a novelty shop.

In fact, a rockcrafter who has mastered most of the designs in this book can produce animals, insects, and people that will add that special touch to your home or to most any party, luncheon, or banquet. Don't be bashful—be bold! Give others a chance to enjoy your rock creatures. After all, your long hours of gathering, gluing, and painting rocks have earned you a secure place in the spotlight.

A GALLERY OF ADDITIONAL CREATIONS

(Above) *Two mallards rest on shelves made from discarded items found at an abandoned silver mine.*

(Below) *The bright colors of this patchwork turtle compliment those of the room whose door she holds open.*

This brown pelican, special ordered as a memento of a Florida visit, is an instant conversation piece.

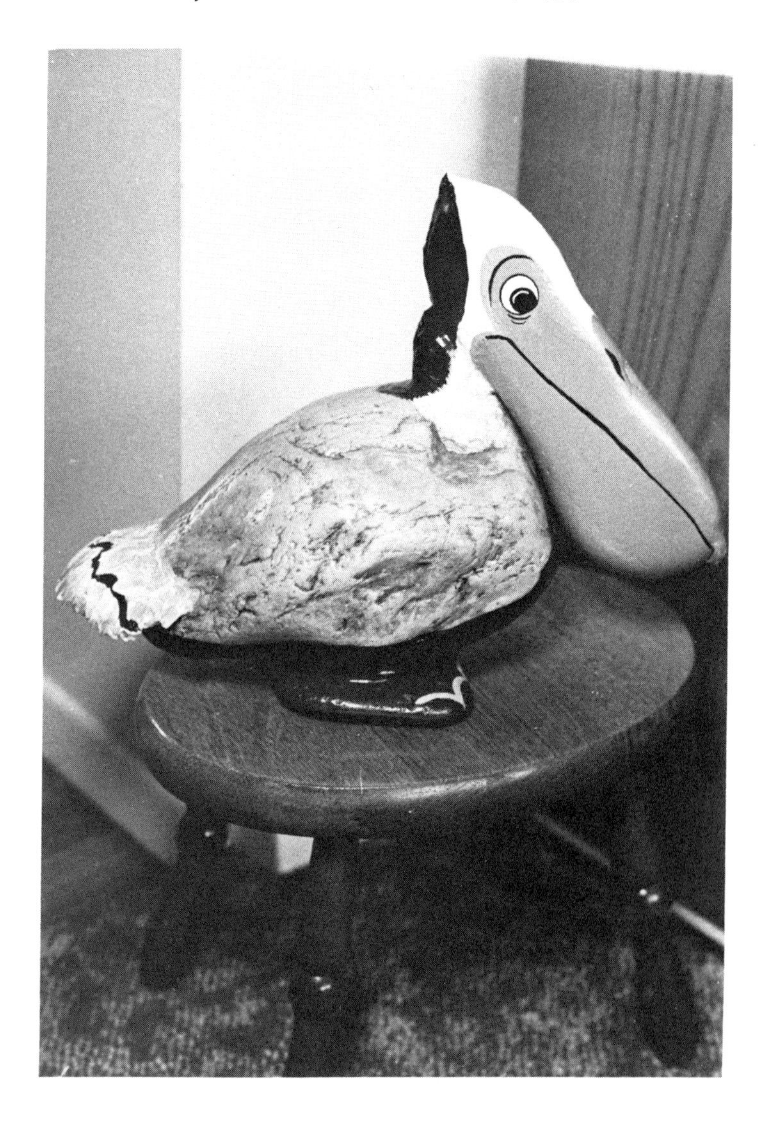

This large frog guards a backyard goldfish pond.

A mischievous elf, perched on a giant rockcrafted mushroom, peers from this flower bed.

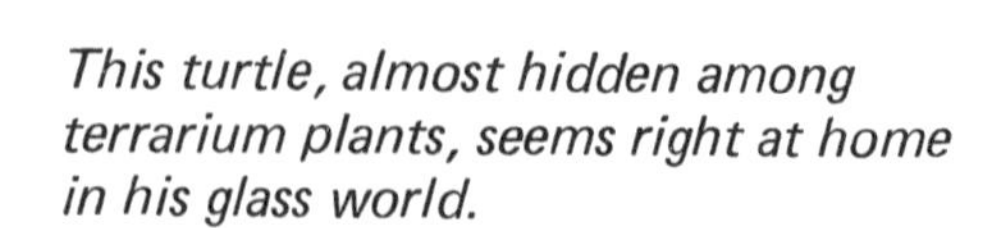

This turtle, almost hidden among terrarium plants, seems right at home in his glass world.

(Above) A large owl adds interest to this stone and brick hearth area.

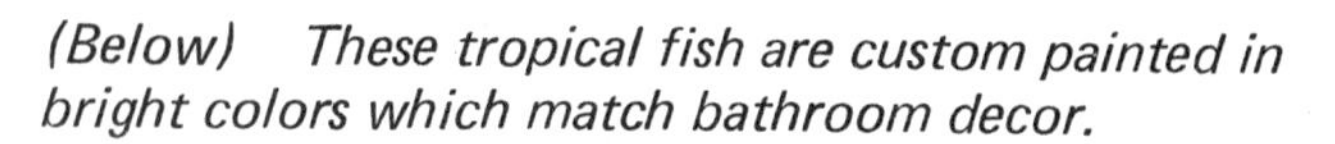

(Below) These tropical fish are custom painted in bright colors which match bathroom decor.

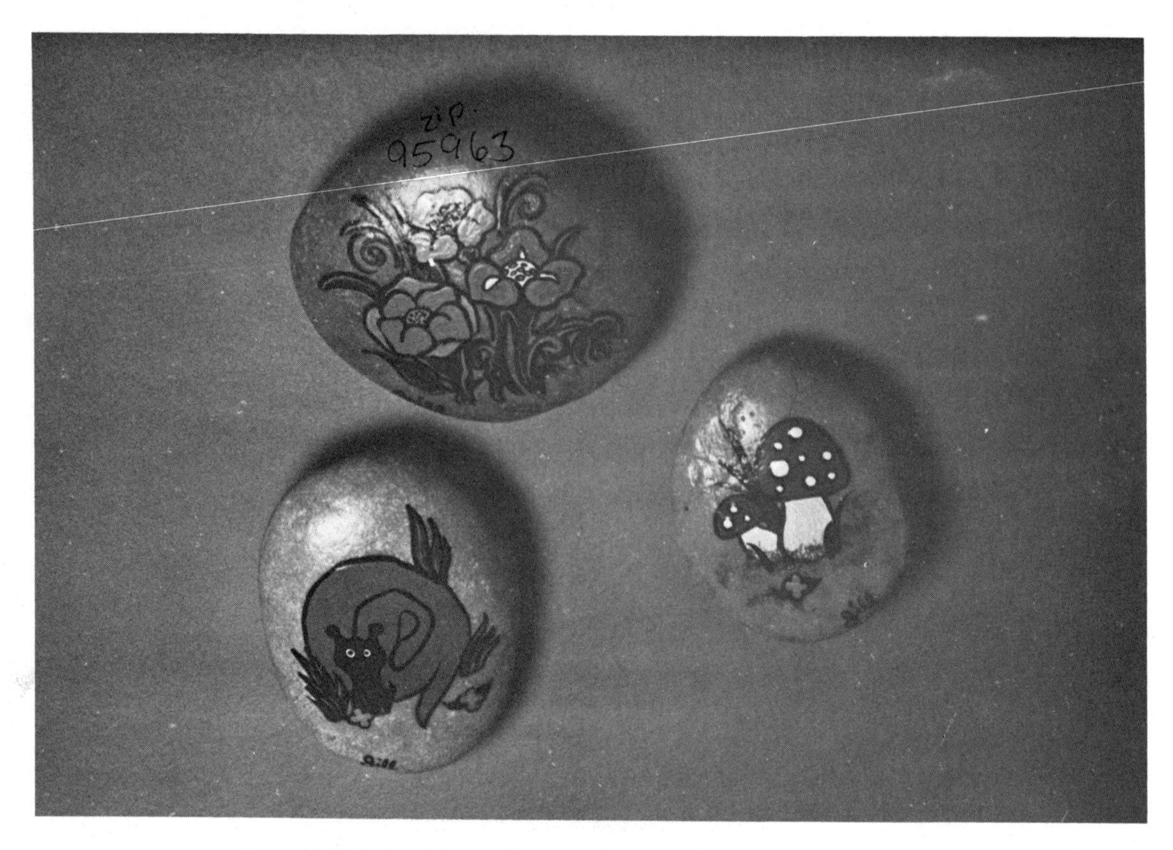

(Above) These flat, oval rocks feature painted flowers, mushrooms, and a snail.

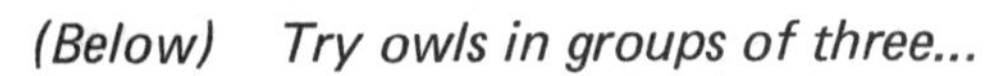

(Below) Try owls in groups of three...

... or in combination with other wall hangings.

This miniature owl, made from a small flat rock, features rock eyes and beak, modeling paste feathers, and an antiqued finish.

This pastel pink elephant adorns a nursery wall.

Beard and fur trim of modeling paste highlight this eleven-rock Santa.

(Above) An owl surrounded by pumpkin coasters makes an unusual Halloween centerpiece.

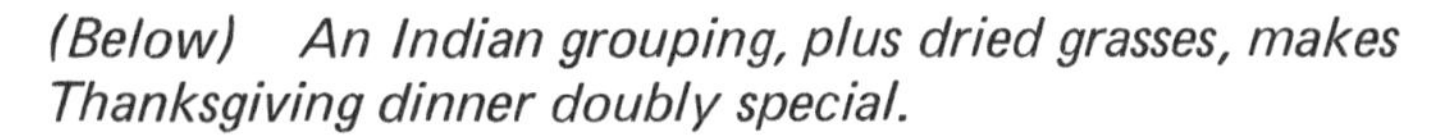

(Below) An Indian grouping, plus dried grasses, makes Thanksgiving dinner doubly special.

This Eskimo grouping is the ideal centerpiece for a summer party featuring baked Alaska served on clear, icy crystal.

This Styrofoam valentine centerpiece is covered in pink felt, trimmed in white lace, and topped by white hearts, a pair of valentine turtles, and a vial holding a tiny red rose.

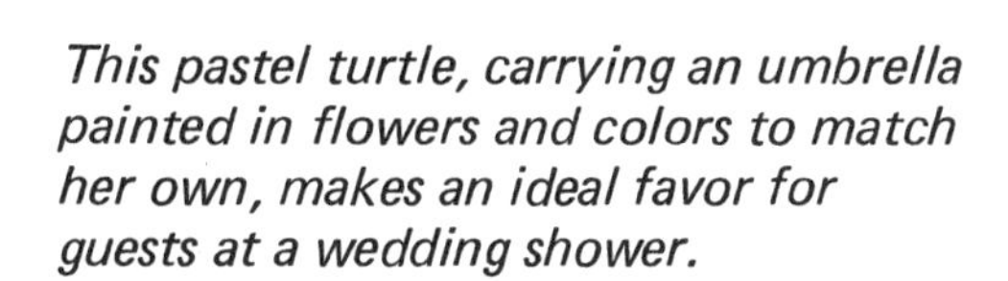

This pastel turtle, carrying an umbrella painted in flowers and colors to match her own, makes an ideal favor for guests at a wedding shower.